D0807620

SALAD DAYS

SALAD DAYS

COLLINS & BROWN

Copyright © The National Magazine Company
Limited and Collins & Brown 2013

All rights reserved. No part of this publication
may be reproduced, stored in a retrieval system,
or transmitted in any form or by any means,
electronic, mechanical, photocopying, recording or
otherwise, without the prior written consent of the
copyright holder.

The expression Good Housekeeping as used in the
title of the book is the trademark of The National
Magazine Company and The Hearst Corporation,
registered in the United Kingdom and USA, and
other principal countries of the world, and is the
absolute property of The National Magazine
Company and The Hearst Corporation. The use
of this trademark other than with the express
permission of The National Magazine Company
or The Hearst Corporation is strictly prohibited.

The Good Housekeeping website is
www.goodhousekeeping.co.uk

ISBN 978-1-908449-99-3

A catalogue record for this book is available from
the British Library.

Reproduction by Dot Gradations Ltd, UK
Printed and bound by
1010 Printing International Ltd, China

This book can be ordered direct from the publisher.
Contact the marketing department, but try your
bookshop first.

www.anovabooks.com

NOTES
Both metric and imperial measures are given for
the recipes. Follow either set of measures, not a
mixture of both, as they are not interchangeable.

All spoon measures are level.
1 tsp = 5ml spoon; 1 tbsp = 15ml spoon.

Ovens and grills must be preheated to the specified
temperature.

Medium eggs should be used except where
otherwise specified. Free-range eggs are
recommended.

Note that some recipes contain raw or lightly
cooked eggs. The young, elderly, pregnant women
and anyone with an immune-deficiency disease
should avoid these because of the slight risk of
salmonella.

Contents

Side Salads

Take 5 Quick Salad Dressings

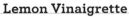

Lemon Vinaigrette

To make about 150ml (¼ pint), you will need:
2 tbsp lemon juice, 2 tsp runny honey, 8 tbsp extra virgin olive oil, 3 tbsp freshly chopped mint, 4 tbsp roughly chopped flat-leafed parsley, salt and freshly ground black pepper.

1. Put the lemon juice, honey and salt and ground black pepper to taste into a small bowl and whisk to combine. Gradually whisk in the oil and stir in the herbs.
2. If not using immediately, store in a cool place and whisk briefly before using.

Lemon and Parsley

To make about 100ml (3½fl oz), you will need:
juice of ½ lemon, 6 tbsp extra virgin olive oil, 4 tbsp freshly chopped flat-leafed parsley, salt and freshly ground black pepper.

1. Put the lemon juice, oil and parsley into a medium bowl and whisk to combine. Season to taste with salt and ground black pepper.
2. If not using immediately, store in a cool place and whisk briefly before using.

Blue Cheese

To make 100ml (3½fl oz), you will need:
50g (2oz) Roquefort cheese, 2 tbsp low-fat yogurt, 1 tbsp white wine vinegar, 5 tbsp extra virgin olive oil, salt and freshly ground black pepper.

1. Crumble the cheese into a food processor or blender with the yogurt, vinegar and oil. Whiz for 1 minute or until thoroughly combined. Season to taste.

2 If not using immediately, store in a cool place and use within one day. Whisk briefly before using.

Chilli Lime

To make 125ml (4fl oz), you will need:

¼ seeded and finely chopped red chilli (see Safety Tip, page 142), 1 crushed garlic clove, 1cm (½in) piece fresh root ginger, peeled and finely grated, juice of 1½ large limes, 50ml (2fl oz) olive oil, 1½ tbsp light muscovado sugar, 2 tbsp fresh coriander leaves, 2 tbsp fresh mint leaves.

1 Put the chilli, garlic, ginger, lime juice, oil and sugar into a food processor or blender and whiz for 10 seconds to combine. Add the coriander and mint and whiz together for 5 seconds to chop roughly.

2 If not using immediately, store in a cool place and use within two days. Whisk briefly before using.

Garlic, Soy and Honey

To make about 100ml (3½fl oz), you will need:

1 crushed garlic clove, 2 tsp each soy sauce and runny honey, 1 tbsp cider vinegar, 4 tbsp olive oil, freshly ground black pepper.

1 Put the garlic into a small bowl. Add the soy sauce, honey, vinegar and oil, season to taste with ground black pepper and whisk to combine.

2 If not using immediately, store in a cool place and whisk briefly before using.

Classic Coleslaw

Hands-on time: 15 minutes

¼ each medium red and white
   cabbage, shredded

1 carrot, grated

20g (¾ oz) fresh flat-leafed parsley,
   finely chopped

For the dressing
1½ tbsp red wine vinegar

4 tbsp olive oil

½ tsp Dijon mustard

salt and freshly ground black pepper

1 To make the dressing, put the
  vinegar into a small bowl, add the
  oil and mustard, season well with
  salt and ground black pepper and
  mix well.

2 Put the cabbage and carrot into a
  large bowl and toss to mix well. Add
  the parsley.

3 Mix the dressing again, pour over
  the cabbage mixture and toss well
  to coat.

SAVE EFFORT

An easy way to get a brand new
dish is to make a **Thai-style
Coleslaw:** replace the red cabbage
with a good handful of fresh
bean sprouts, and the parsley
with freshly chopped coriander.
Add 1 seeded and finely chopped
red chilli (see Safety Tip, page
142). For the dressing, replace the
vinegar with lime juice, the olive
oil with toasted sesame oil and the
mustard with soy sauce.

Light and Fresh Potato Salad

Hands-on time: 15 minutes
Cooking time: about 20 minutes

1.5kg (3lb 2oz) new potatoes, unpeeled, chopped into bite-size pieces
100ml (3½fl oz) olive oil
2 tbsp wholegrain mustard
juice of ½ lemon
200g (7oz) radishes, thinly sliced
4 spring onions, thinly sliced
a punnet of cress
salt and freshly ground black pepper

1 Cook the potatoes in salted boiling water for 15–20 minutes until just tender but not breaking apart.
2 While the potatoes are cooking, whisk together the oil, mustard, lemon juice and plenty of seasoning.
3 Drain the potatoes and leave to steam-dry for 5 minutes, then put them back into the pan. Pour the dressing over and add the radishes and spring onions. Fold together, trying not to break up the potatoes.
4 Tip into a serving dish and scatter the leaves from a punnet of cress over the top.

SAVE TIME

Prepare the potato salad up to a couple of hours ahead, but do not add the cress. Transfer to a serving dish, cover with clingfilm and chill. Complete the recipe to serve.

Serves 12

Tomato and Onion Salad

Hands-on time: 15 minutes, plus standing

500g (1lb 2oz) baby plum tomatoes, halved

1 bunch of spring onions, sliced

500g (1lb 2oz) plum tomatoes, sliced lengthways

a handful of fresh basil leaves, roughly torn, plus sprigs to garnish

2 beef tomatoes (total weight about 450g/1lb), sliced

100g (3½oz) pinenuts, toasted

250g (9oz) medium tomatoes, cut into wedges

salt and freshly ground black pepper

For the dressing

100ml (3½fl oz) extra virgin olive oil

50ml (2fl oz) balsamic vinegar

a pinch of golden caster sugar

1 Put all the ingredients for the dressing into a screw-topped jar, then season generously with salt and ground black pepper. Shake well to combine.

2 Layer the baby plum tomatoes, spring onions, plum tomatoes, basil, beef tomatoes, pinenuts and, finally, the medium tomatoes in a shallow serving bowl, seasoning each layer with salt and pepper.

3 Drizzle the dressing over the salad and put to one side for 1 hour to allow the flavours to mingle. Garnish with basil sprigs to serve.

SAVE EFFORT

For a simple tomato and basil salad, omit the spring onions and pinenuts, and reduce the quantity of dressing by one-third.

Serves 4

Perfect Tomatoes

Tomatoes and full-flavoured Mediterranean vegetable fruits such as aubergines and peppers add a rich flavour to many dishes. Each have their individual preparation techniques. Follow the steps below for perfect tomato preparation.

Seeding tomatoes

1 Halve the tomato through the core. Using a spoon or a small sharp knife, remove the seeds and juice, then shake off the excess liquid.

2 Chop the tomato as required for your recipe and place in a colander for a minute or two, to drain off any excess liquid.

SAVE TIME

If you are using tomatoes in a sauce that will be cooked for a long time, you can just roughly chop them without peeling and then, if you prefer it smooth, sieve the sauce after cooking

1

Peeling tomatoes

1 Fill a bowl or pan with boiling water. Using a slotted spoon, carefully add the tomato and leave for 15–30 seconds, then put on a chopping board.

2 Using a small sharp knife, cut out the core in a single cone-shaped piece. Discard the core.

3 Peel off the skin; it should come away easily, depending on ripeness.

White Bean Salad

Hands-on time: 15 minutes

½ tbsp red wine vinegar

2 tbsp extra virgin olive oil

½ red cabbage

2 courgettes

400g can cannellini beans, drained and rinsed

400g can butter beans, drained and rinsed

½ red onion, finely chopped

100g (3½oz) stale unsliced bread, torn into small chunks

125g ball low-fat mozzarella, torn into small pieces

a handful of fresh basil leaves, chopped

salt and freshly ground black pepper

1 Whisk together the vinegar, oil, plenty of seasoning and a splash of water in a small bowl to make a dressing.

2 Cut out and discard the tough core from the cabbage, then finely shred the leaves and put into a large serving bowl. Peel the courgettes into ribbons, using a Y-shaped peeler, and add to the cabbage bowl. Add the remaining ingredients and the dressing and toss well to combine. Serve.

Serves 4

Pea Salad

🍴 **Hands-on time:** 10 minutes
Cooking time: 5 minutes

400g (14oz) fresh or frozen peas
grated zest and juice of 1 lemon
2 tbsp extra virgin olive oil
1–1½ tbsp wholegrain mustard, to taste
a small handful of fresh mint, roughly
    chopped
a large handful of rocket, torn
salt and freshly ground black pepper

1 Fill a large bowl with ice-cold water.
  Bring a large pan of water to the
  boil, add the peas, then bring back
  to the boil and cook for 1 minute.
  Drain, then plunge the peas into the
  iced water to cool. Drain again and
  put into a bowl.
2 Put the lemon zest and juice, oil
  and mustard into a jug with some
  seasoning and whisk to combine.
3 Toss the dressing, mint and rocket
  through the peas. Check the
  seasoning and serve.

SAVE TIME

Complete steps 1 and 2 up to one
day ahead. Cover the peas and
dressing separately with clingfilm.
Complete step 3 to serve.

Serves 6

Grated Beetroot Salad

Hands-on time: 15 minutes

3 large carrots, coarsely grated
500g (1lb 2oz) raw beetroot
finely grated zest and juice of
   1 large orange
1½ tbsp runny honey
1 eating apple
50g (2oz) walnuts, roughly chopped
a few caperberries
a small handful of fresh flat-leafed
   parsley, roughly chopped
salt and freshly ground black pepper

1 Put the carrots into one half of a serving bowl. Wearing kitchen gloves to stop your hands getting stained, peel and coarsely grate the beetroot, then put into the other half of the bowl.

2 Mix the orange zest and juice, honey and some seasoning together in a small bowl.

3 Finely dice the apple (keeping the skin on) and scatter over the grated vegetables, together with the chopped walnuts, caperberries and parsley. Drizzle the dressing over and serve.

SAVE TIME

Prepare the salad to the end of step 1 up to 1 hour in advance. Cover and chill the vegetables. Complete step 2, cover the dressing and keep at room temperature. Complete step 3 to serve.

Serves 6

Herb Vinegar

To make 600ml (1 pint), you will need:
25g (1oz) fresh herbs, plus extra sprigs for bottling, 600ml (1 pint) red or white wine vinegar.

1 Put the herbs and vinegar into a pan and bring to the boil. Pour into a heatproof bowl, cover and leave overnight.
2 Strain through a muslin-lined sieve and bottle with herb sprigs. Store for one week before using.

Mint Yogurt Dressing

To make about 175ml (6fl oz), you will need:
150g (5oz) Greek yogurt, 3-4 tbsp freshly chopped mint leaves, 2 tbsp extra virgin olive oil, salt and freshly ground black pepper.

1 Put the yogurt into a bowl and add the mint and oil. Season to taste with salt and ground black pepper and stir to combine.

2 If not using immediately, store in a cool place and use within one day. Whisk briefly before using.

Mustard Dressing

To make about 100ml (3½fl oz), you will need:
1 tbsp wholegrain mustard, juice of ½ lemon, 6 tbsp extra virgin olive oil, salt and freshly ground black pepper.

1 Put the mustard, lemon juice and oil into a small bowl and whisk to combine. Season to taste with salt and ground black pepper.

2 If not using immediately, store in a cool place and whisk briefly before using.

Sun-dried Tomato Dressing

To make about 100ml (3½fl oz), you will need:
2 sun-dried tomatoes in oil, drained, 2 tbsp oil from sun-dried tomato jar, 2 tbsp red wine vinegar, 1 garlic clove, 1 tbsp sun-dried tomato paste, a pinch of sugar (optional), 2 tbsp extra virgin olive oil, salt and freshly ground black pepper.

1 Put the sun-dried tomatoes and oil, the vinegar, garlic and tomato paste into a blender or food processor. Add the sugar, if you like.
2 With the motor running, pour the oil through the feeder tube and whiz briefly to make a fairly thick dressing. Season to taste with salt and ground black pepper.
3 If not using immediately, store in a cool place and whisk briefly before using.

Fruit Vinegar

To make 600ml (1 pint), you will need:
450g (1lb) raspberries and blackberries, plus extra for bottling, 600ml (1 pint) red wine vinegar.

1 Put the fruit into a bowl and, using the back of a spoon, break it up, then add the vinegar. Cover and leave to stand three days, stirring now and then.
2 Strain through a muslin-lined sieve and bottle with extra fruits. Store for two weeks before using.

2

Salad Caprese

Hands-on time: 10 minutes

3 × 150g balls buffalo mozzarella,
   drained

1kg (2¼lb) very ripe tomatoes, sliced
   into rounds

extra virgin olive oil to drizzle

a small handful of fresh basil leaves,
   roughly shredded

sea salt and freshly ground
   black pepper

1 Slice the mozzarella into rounds and layer on a serving plate with the tomato slices.

2 Drizzle with the oil, season with sea salt and ground black pepper and scatter the basil over.

Serves 4

Waldorf Salad

450g (1lb) eating apples, peeled
 and cored
juice of ½ lemon
1 tsp sugar
150ml (¼ pint) mayonnaise (see
 page 150)
1 lettuce
½ head of celery, sliced
50g (2oz) walnut pieces, chopped
a few walnut halves to garnish
 (optional)

1 Slice one apple and dice the rest. Dip
the slices into lemon juice to prevent
discoloration. Toss the diced apples
in the lemon juice, the sugar and
1 tbsp of the mayonnaise and leave
to stand for about 30 minutes.

2 Just before serving, line a salad
bowl with lettuce leaves. Add the
celery, walnuts and remaining
mayonnaise to the diced apples and
toss together. Spoon into the salad
bowl and garnish with the apple
slices, and a few whole walnuts, if
you like.

Serves 4

Crunchy Ribbon Salad

Hands-on time: 10 minutes

2 large carrots, trimmed
1 cucumber
1 courgette
2 tbsp sweet chilli sauce
1 tbsp white wine vinegar
salt and freshly ground black pepper

1 Use a vegetable peeler to make carrot ribbons. Put the ribbons into a large bowl. Trim the cucumber and courgette and peel both into ribbons. Add to the carrots.
2 Pour the sweet chilli sauce and vinegar over the vegetables and season. Use your hands to toss everything together. Serve immediately.

SAVE TIME

Complete step 1 up to 2 hours ahead. Cover with damp kitchen paper, then chill. Bring to room temperature, then complete step 2 to serve.

Serves 6

Summer Vegetable Salad

Hands-on time: 10 minutes
Cooking time: about 7 minutes

600g (1lb 5oz) mixed green
    vegetables, such as green beans,
    peas, sugarsnap peas, trimmed
    asparagus, broad beans, broccoli
¼ small cucumber, halved lengthways,
    seeded and sliced
2 tbsp freshly chopped flat-leafed
    parsley

For the dressing
1 tbsp white wine vinegar or
    sherry vinegar
1 tsp English mustard powder
3 tbsp extra virgin olive oil
salt and freshly ground black pepper

1 Cook the green beans in a large pan
of salted boiling water for 3 minutes,
then add all the other vegetables.
Bring the water back to the boil and
cook for a further 3–4 minutes. Drain
and put immediately into a bowl of
ice-cold water. Drain well.

2 Whisk all the dressing ingredients
together with some seasoning. Toss
the vegetables in the dressing with
the cucumber and parsley.

SAVE EFFORT

An easy way to get a brand new
dish is to change the dressing:
Yogurt Dressing: mix together
5 tbsp natural yogurt with 1 tbsp
each freshly chopped mint and
chives and 1 small crushed garlic
clove. Season with salt and freshly
ground black pepper.
Tomato Dressing: halve and seed
8 cherry tomatoes and cut into
thin strips. Mix 1 tbsp balsamic
vinegar with 3 tbsp olive oil, 2 tbsp
freshly chopped tarragon, salt and
freshly ground black pepper. Stir
in the tomato and drizzle over the
vegetables.

Serves 4

Veggie Salads

Broad Bean and Feta Salad

Hands-on time: 10 minutes
Cooking time: 5 minutes, plus cooling

225g (8oz) podded broad beans (see
   Save Effort)
100g (3½oz) feta cheese, chopped
2 tbsp freshly chopped mint
2 tbsp extra virgin olive oil
a squeeze of lemon juice
salt and freshly ground black pepper
lemon wedges to serve (optional)

1 Cook the beans in salted boiling
water for 3–5 minutes until tender.
Drain, then plunge them into cold
water and drain again. Remove their
skins if you like (see Save Effort).

2 Tip the beans into a bowl and add
the feta, mint, oil and a squeeze of
lemon juice. Season well with salt
and ground black pepper and toss
together. Serve with lemon wedges,
if you like.

SAVE EFFORT

For this quantity of broad beans,
you will need to buy about 750g
(1½lb) beans in pods. Choose
small pods, as the beans will
be young and will have a better
flavour than bigger, older beans.
Very young broad beans, less
than 7.5cm (3in) long, can be
cooked in their pods and eaten
whole. Pod older beans and skin
them to remove the outer coat,
which toughens with age. To do
this, slip the beans out of their
skins after blanching.

Serves 2

Goat's Cheese and Walnut Salad

🍴 **Hands-on time:** 10 minutes

1 large radicchio, shredded
2 bunches of prepared watercress
   (total weight about 125g/4oz)
1 red onion, finely sliced
150g (5oz) walnut pieces
200g (7oz) goat's cheese, crumbled

For the dressing
2 tbsp red wine vinegar
8 tbsp olive oil
a large pinch of caster sugar
salt and freshly ground black pepper

1 Whisk all the ingredients for the dressing together in a small bowl and put to one side.
2 Put the radicchio, watercress and onion into a large bowl. Pour the dressing over and toss well.
3 To serve, divide the salad among six serving plates and sprinkle the walnuts and goat's cheese on top.

Serves 6

Panzanella

Hands-on time: 20 minutes, plus standing

2–3 thick slices from a day-old country loaf (total weight about 100g/3½oz), torn or cut into cubes

450g (1lb) ripe tomatoes, roughly chopped

2 tbsp capers

1 tsp freshly chopped thyme

1 small red onion, thinly sliced

2 garlic cloves

2 small red chillies, seeded and finely chopped (see Safety Tip, page 142)

4 tbsp extra virgin olive oil

125g (4oz) pitted black olives

50g (2oz) sun-dried tomatoes, roughly chopped

8 fresh basil leaves

25g (1oz) Parmesan, pared into shavings with a vegetable peeler

salt and freshly ground black pepper

fresh thyme sprigs to garnish

1 Put the bread into a large bowl with the tomatoes, capers, chopped thyme, onion, garlic, chillies, oil, olives and sun-dried tomatoes. Season well with salt and ground black pepper, then toss together and leave in a cool place for 30 minutes.

2 Toss the salad thoroughly again. Tear the basil into pieces and scatter over the salad with the Parmesan shavings. Garnish with thyme sprigs, then serve.

SAVE TIME

This salad is best made two or three hours ahead to let the flavours mingle.

Serves 4

Grilled Ciabatta and Mozzarella Salad

Hands-on time: 10 minutes
Cooking time: 5 minutes

8 thick slices Italian bread, such as ciabatta
2 tsp olive paste or sun-dried tomato paste
2 × 150g packs of mozzarella cheese, drained and sliced
4 tbsp olive oil, plus extra to drizzle
2 tbsp balsamic vinegar
280g jar artichoke hearts in oil, drained and sliced (see Save Effort)
100g (3½oz) rocket salad
50g (2oz) sun-dried tomato halves
salt and freshly ground black pepper

1 Preheat the grill. Toast the bread slices on one side. Spread the untoasted side with olive or sun-dried tomato paste, then top with mozzarella slices and drizzle lightly with oil.

2 Mix the vinegar, salt and ground black pepper in a bowl and whisk in the 4 tbsp oil. Add the sliced artichoke hearts.

3 Grill the bread slices for 2–3 minutes until the mozzarella browns lightly.

4 Toss the rocket salad with the artichoke mixture and divide among four plates. Top with two slices of grilled bread and the sun-dried tomatoes.

SAVE EFFORT

Find marinated artichokes in supermarkets; alternatively, buy canned artichoke hearts, drain, slice and cover in olive oil. They will keep in the fridge for up to one week.

Serves 4

For The Slice: Avocados

Prepare avocados just before serving because their flesh discolours quickly once exposed to air.

1. Halve the avocado lengthways and twist the two halves apart. Tap the stone with a sharp knife, then twist the knife to remove the stone.

2. Run a knife between the flesh and skin and peel the skin away. Slice the flesh.

Understanding Cheese

Vegetarian Cheese

The traditional rennet used to separate milk into firm curds and liquid whey comes from the stomach lining of a young calf. Cheeses suitable for vegetarians are made using a non-animal rennet substitute, from either the bacteria *Bacillus subtilis* or *Bacillus prodigiosum*, the fungus *Mucor miehei*, or certain plants. Some traditional cheeses have always been made using natural rennets, including fig juice, melon, wild thistle and safflower.

Other cheeses, such as Parmesan, for example, are always made using animal rennet, because of European Union regulations for their production and labelling.

However, a 'Parmesan-style hard cheese' is suitable for vegetarians and a wide variety of cheeses now made with non-animal rennet are labelled as suitable for vegetarians. There is no particular type of cheese that is exclusively vegetarian and soft cheeses are as likely to be non-vegetarian as hard cheese. Always check the label.

Halloumi and Avocado Salad

Hands-on time: 10 minutes
Cooking time: 5 minutes

250g (9oz) halloumi cheese, sliced into eight (see Healthy Tip)
1 tbsp plain flour, seasoned
2 tbsp olive oil
200g (7oz) mixed leaf salad
2 avocados, halved, stoned, peeled and sliced
fresh rocket leaves to garnish
lemon halves to serve

For the mint dressing

3 tbsp lemon juice
8 tbsp olive oil
3 tbsp freshly chopped mint
salt and freshly ground black pepper

1 To make the dressing, whisk the lemon juice with the oil and mint, then season with salt and ground black pepper.
2 Coat the halloumi with the seasoned flour. Heat the oil in a large frying pan and fry the cheese for 1 minute on each side or until it forms a golden crust.
3 Meanwhile, put the salad leaves and avocado into a large bowl, add half the dressing and toss together. Arrange the hot cheese on top and drizzle the remaining dressing over. Garnish with rocket leaves and serve with lemon halves to squeeze over.

HEALTHY TIP

Some vegetarians prefer to avoid cheeses that have been produced by the traditional method, because this uses animal-derived rennet; however, most supermarkets and cheese shops now stock an excellent range of vegetarian cheeses, produced using vegetarian rennet. Always check the label when buying.

Serves 4

Warm Salad with Quorn and Berries

Hands-on time: 5 minutes
Cooking time: 12 minutes

2 tbsp olive oil
1 onion, sliced
175g pack of Quorn pieces
2 tbsp raspberry vinegar
150g (5oz) blueberries
225g (8oz) mixed salad leaves
salt and freshly ground black pepper

1 Heat the oil in a frying pan, add the onion and cook for 5 minutes or until soft and golden. Increase the heat and add the Quorn pieces. Cook, stirring, for 5 minutes or until golden brown. Season with salt and ground black pepper, then place in a large bowl and put to one side.

2 Add the vinegar, 75ml (3fl oz) water and the blueberries to the frying pan. Bring to the boil and bubble for 1–2 minutes until it reaches a syrupy consistency.

3 Toss the Quorn, blueberry mixture and salad leaves gently together. Serve immediately.

Serves 4

Warm Tofu, Fennel and Bean Salad

Hands-on time: 10 minutes
Cooking time: about 15 minutes

1 tbsp olive oil, plus 1 tsp

1 red onion, finely sliced

1 fennel bulb, finely sliced

1 tbsp cider vinegar

400g can butter beans, drained and rinsed

2 tbsp freshly chopped flat-leafed parsley

200g (7oz) smoked tofu, sliced lengthways into eight

salt and freshly ground black pepper

1 Heat the 1 tbsp oil in a large frying pan. Add the onion and fennel and cook over a medium heat for 5–10 minutes. Add the vinegar and heat through for 2 minutes, then stir in the butter beans and parsley. Season with salt and ground black pepper, then tip into a bowl.

2 Add the tofu to the pan with the remaining oil. Cook for 2 minutes on each side or until golden. Divide the bean mixture among four plates and add two slices of tofu to each plate.

Feel-good
Salads

Understanding Nutrients

A quick and easy way to assess if a food is high or low in a particular nutrient is to use the table opposite. Look at the amount of a particular nutrient per serving or per 100g (3½oz) for snacks or cooking ingredients and check the table to find out if it's high or low.

'We are what we eat'

Nutritionists from around the world agree that the food we eat has an important effect on our health and vitality. From the moment of conception and throughout life, diet plays a crucial role in helping us maintain health and fitness. A healthy balanced diet can protect against serious illnesses such as heart disease and cancer, increase resistance to colds and other infections, boost energy levels, help combat the stresses of modern living and also improve physical and mental performance. So, eating a diet that is healthy, varied and tasty should be everyone's aim.

Choose wisely

Our body needs over 40 different nutrients to function and stay healthy. Some, such as carbohydrates, proteins and fats, are required in relatively large amounts; others, such as vitamins, minerals and trace elements, are required in minute amounts, but are nonetheless essential for health. No single food or food group provides all the nutrients we need, which is why we need to eat a variety of different foods. Making sure your body gets all the nutrients it needs is easy if you focus on foods that are nutrient rich and dump those highly refined and processed foods that provide lots of saturated fat, sugar and calories but not much else.

	High	Low
Fat	more than 20g	less than 3g
Saturated fat	more than 5g	less than 1g
Sugar	more than 10g	less than 2g
Fibre	more than 3g	less than 0.5g
Sodium	more than 0.5g	less than 0.1g
Salt	more than 1.3g	less than 0.3g

GDAs (Guideline Daily Amounts)			
	Women	Men	Children (5–10 years)
Energy (calories)	2,000	2,500	1,800
Protein (g)	45	55	24
Carbohydrate (g)	230	300	220
Fat (g)	70	95	70
Saturated fat (g)	20	30	20
Total sugars (g)	90	120	85
Dietary fibre (g)	24	24	15
Sodium (g)	2.4	2.4	1.6
Salt (g)	6	6	4

Smoked Mackerel Superfood Salad

Hands-on time: 15 minutes

1 red grapefruit

½–1 tbsp wholegrain mustard, to taste

1 tbsp rapeseed oil

175g (6oz) smoked mackerel, skinned and flaked

300g (11oz) raw tenderstem broccoli, thinly sliced lengthways

400g can lentils, drained and rinsed

100g (3½oz) pomegranate seeds

100g bag watercress

25g (1oz) pumpkin seeds

salt and freshly ground black pepper

1 Slice the top and bottom off the grapefruit and sit it on a board. Using a small serrated knife, cut away the peel and white pith. Hold the grapefruit over a small bowl and cut between the membranes to separate the segments. Squeeze the membranes into a separate small bowl to extract as much juice as possible (add any extra juice from the segment bowl).

2 Whisk the mustard, oil and plenty of seasoning into the juice bowl to make a dressing.

3 Put all the remaining ingredients into a large bowl and toss together. Drizzle the dressing over and add the grapefruit segments. Toss carefully together and serve.

Serves 4

Hot-smoked Salmon Salad

Hands-on time: 15 minutes
Cooking time: 8 minutes

4 medium eggs
300g (11oz) small new potatoes, quartered
200g (7oz) fine green beans, trimmed and halved
100g (3½oz) radishes, thinly sliced
80g bag salad leaves
50g (2oz) ready-made croûtons
250g (9oz) hot-smoked salmon, skinned and flaked
lemon wedges to serve

For the dressing

3 tbsp sweet chilli sauce
1 tbsp freshly chopped chives
2 tbsp extra virgin olive oil
salt and freshly ground black pepper

1 Bring two small pans of water to the boil. To one, add the eggs and simmer for 7 minutes. To the other, add the potatoes and beans and cook for 6 minutes or until just tender.

2 Meanwhile, put the radishes into a large bowl with the salad leaves, croûtons and salmon flakes. Whisk all the dressing ingredients together in a small bowl with some seasoning.

3 Drain the potatoes and beans and leave to steam-dry in a colander. Lift out the eggs and run them under cold water, then shell and quarter. Add the potatoes and beans to the salad bowl and toss gently.

4 Divide the salad mixture among four plates and top each with a quartered egg. Drizzle the dressing over and serve with lemon wedges.

Serves 4

Take 5 Understanding Fat

Of all the nutrients in our diet, fat must be the most debated and the most misunderstood. Although, in terms of healthy eating, fat is often cast as the villain, it's worth remembering that it also plays a beneficial role. In the body, fat cushions and protects the vital organs, provides energy stores and helps insulate the body. In the diet, it is necessary for the absorption of fat-soluble vitamins (A, D, E and K) and to provide essential fatty acids that the body can't make itself. While some fat is essential, many of us are eating too much of the wrong types of fat and not enough of the right types. A high-fat diet, particularly one that contains a lot of saturated 'animal' fats, is known to increase the risk of problems such as heart disease, stroke and certain types of cancer. There are three types of fat: saturated, monounsaturated and polyunsaturated fatty acids, which occur in different proportions in foods. Saturated fatty acids are linked to higher blood cholesterol, which can then lead to heart disease.

Polyunsaturated fats
Omega-6 fats These are mostly found in margarines and vegetable oils such as sunflower oil, safflower oil, corn oil and soya bean oil. Omega-6 fats help lower the LDL ('bad') cholesterol in the blood, but if you eat too much they will also lower the 'good'.

HDL cholesterol
Omega-3 fats These are found mainly in oil-rich fish such as salmon, fresh tuna, mackerel and sardines, in linseeds (flax) and rapeseed oil. They help to protect the heart by making the blood less sticky and likely to clot, by lowering blood pressure and by encouraging the muscles lining the artery walls to relax, thus improving blood flow to the heart. It's important to have

a balance of omega-3 and omega-6 fats in the diet. At the moment most of us have too much omega-6 fats and not enough omega-3 fats and recent research suggests that low levels of omega-3s in the blood may contribute to depression, antisocial behaviour and schizophrenia.

Monounsaturated fats

Monounsaturated fats are found mainly in olive oil, walnut oil and rapeseed oil, nuts and avocados. They can help reduce the risk of heart disease by lowering LDL ('bad') cholesterol.

Saturated fats

Saturated 'animal' fats are found in full-fat dairy products (cheese, yogurt, milk, cream), lard, fatty cuts of meat and meat products such as sausages and burgers, pastry, cakes, biscuits, and coconut and palm oil. A diet high in saturated fats can raise levels of LDL ('bad') cholesterol in the blood, which will cause narrowing of the arteries and increase the risk of heart attacks and stroke.

Trans fats

Trans fats occur naturally in small amounts in meat and dairy products, but they are also produced during the process of hydrogenation that is used to convert liquid vegetable oils into semi-solid fats in the manufacture of some types of margarine. Trans fats are most commonly found in biscuits, cakes, pastries, meat pies, sausages, crackers and takeaway foods. Although, chemically, trans fats are still unsaturated fat, studies show that in the body they behave like saturated fat, causing blood cholesterol levels to rise; in fact, some studies suggest that trans fats are worse than saturated fats.

Seared Tuna Salad

Hands-on time: 15 minutes
Cooking time: about 8 minutes

1 tsp olive oil
2 × 240g tuna steaks
200g (7oz) fine green beans
4 Little Gem lettuces, leaves separated
a small handful of fresh mint, roughly
   chopped
100g (3½oz) feta, crumbled
200g (7oz) cherry tomatoes, halved
crusty bread to serve (optional)

For the dressing
finely grated zest and juice of 1 lemon
1 tbsp wholegrain mustard
1 tsp caster sugar
1 tbsp extra virgin olive oil
salt and freshly ground black pepper

1 Heat the oil in a large griddle or frying pan over a high heat and cook the tuna steaks for 5 minutes, turning them midway through (cook for longer/shorter as preferred).

2 Meanwhile, bring a small pan of water to the boil and cook the beans for 5 minutes or until just tender. Drain. Whisk all the dressing ingredients together in a small bowl or jug with some seasoning.

3 When the tuna is cooked to your liking, transfer it to a board and slice. Put the slices into a large serving bowl and add the drained beans, lettuce leaves, mint, crumbled feta, cherry tomatoes and dressing. Toss together and serve with crusty bread, if you like.

SAVE EFFORT

If you like, use ready-to-eat tuna or hot-smoked salmon or mackerel instead of cooking fresh fish.

Serves 4

Herring Curry Salad

Hands-on time: 15 minutes

5 tbsp extra light mayonnaise
5 tbsp half-fat crème fraîche
½ tbsp mild curry powder
1½ tbsp capers, drained and rinsed
finely grated zest of 1 lemon
40g (1½oz) walnuts, finely chopped
1 celery stick, finely chopped
1 apple, cored and finely chopped
1 shallot, finely chopped
a large handful of fresh curly parsley,
  roughly chopped
salt and freshly ground black pepper

To serve

2 × 260g pots rollmops
4 slices rye bread
lemon wedges

1 Put all the salad ingredients into a medium serving bowl and add seasoning to taste.
2 Serve with the rollmops, rye bread and lemon wedges.

Prawn Noodle Salad

Hands-on time: 15 minutes

300g bag cooked rice noodles
juice of 2 limes
1 tbsp fish sauce
2 tsp light soft brown sugar
1 red chilli, seeded and finely chopped
  (see Safety Tip, page 142)
2.5cm (1in) piece fresh root ginger,
  peeled and grated
2 carrots, peeled into ribbons
300g (11oz) bean sprouts
200g (7oz) sugarsnap peas, sliced
350g (12oz) cooked king prawns,
  peeled and deveined
a large handful of fresh mint leaves,
  chopped
40g (1½oz) roasted salted peanuts,
  roughly chopped, to garnish

1 Put the rice noodles into a heatproof bowl and pour boiling water from the kettle over them until they are covered. Leave for 5 minutes to heat through. Drain well and put the noodles back into the bowl.

2 In a separate bowl, stir together the lime juice, fish sauce, sugar, chilli and ginger. Add the vegetables, prawns and mint to the drained noodles, then pour the dressing on and toss through. Garnish with peanuts and serve.

Serves 4

Warm Smoked Salmon and Cucumber Salad

Hands-on time: 10 minutes
Cooking time: about 5 minutes

½ tbsp vegetable oil

2.5cm (1in) piece fresh root ginger, peeled and finely chopped

1 green chilli, seeded and finely chopped (see Safety Tip, page 142)

1 tbsp sesame seeds

6 baby sweetcorn, finely sliced

300g (11oz) straight-to-wok rice noodles

1 cucumber, peeled into ribbons

1 tbsp each toasted sesame oil and soy sauce

120g pack of smoked salmon trimmings

salt and freshly ground black pepper

a large handful of fresh coriander, finely chopped, to garnish

lime wedges to serve

1 Heat the oil in a large frying pan or wok. Add the ginger, chilli and sesame seeds and cook for 1 minute. Stir in the baby sweetcorn and noodles and cook, stirring frequently, for 3 minutes or until the noodles are tender.

2 Add the cucumber, sesame oil, soy sauce and smoked salmon trimmings and heat through. Check the seasoning. Garnish with coriander and serve immediately with lime wedges to squeeze over.

Serves 4

Detox Chicken Salad

½ head of broccoli (weight about 175g/6oz)

4 cooked chicken breasts (total weight about 400g/14oz), shredded

1 medium avocado, halved, stoned, peeled and sliced

125g (4oz) mixed sprouts (sprouting beans and pulses)

410g can black-eyed beans, drained and rinsed

50g (2oz) rocket leaves

3 tbsp extra virgin olive oil

1 tsp wholegrain mustard

2 tsp white wine vinegar

2 tbsp sunflower seeds

salt and freshly ground black pepper

1 Using a sharp knife, shave the florets off the broccoli and put them into a large serving bowl. Next, thinly slice the remaining broccoli stalk and cut it into matchsticks. Add to the bowl. Add the shredded chicken, avocado, mixed sprouts, black-eyed beans and rocket and toss through.

2 In a small bowl, whisk together the oil, mustard, vinegar, seasoning and a splash of water. Toss the dressing gently through the salad, sprinkle the sunflower seeds over and serve.

Serves 4

Crunchy Chicken Salad

Hands-on time: 20 minutes
Cooking time: about 20 minutes, plus cooling

2 × 125g (4oz) skinless chicken breasts
1 large carrot
75g (3oz) sugarsnap peas
1 red pepper, seeded
½ mango, peeled and stoned
a large handful of fresh coriander,
   roughly chopped
15g (½oz) salted peanuts, roughly
   chopped, to garnish

For the dressing

grated zest and juice of 1 lime
¾ tbsp toasted sesame oil
1 tbsp runny honey
1 tsp fish sauce
¾ tsp sesame seeds
salt and freshly ground black pepper

1 Put the chicken breasts into a pan
   and cover with cold water. Bring
   to the boil, then reduce the heat and
   simmer gently for 15 minutes. Take
   off the heat and put to one side for
   10 minutes.

2 Meanwhile, cut the carrot, sugarsnap
   peas, red pepper and mango into
   thin strips. Put the vegetables into a
   large bowl and stir in the mango.

3 Whisk all the dressing ingredients
   together in a small bowl with some
   salt and ground black pepper.

4 Lift the chicken out of the water and,
   when cool enough to handle, shred.
   Add to the vegetable bowl. Add the
   dressing and coriander and toss
   through, then garnish with roughly
   chopped peanuts and serve.

SAVE EFFORT

An easy way to get a brand new
dish is to stir in some cooked egg
noodles in step 4.

Serves 2

Midweek Salads

Keep It Seasonal

Why? Because the produce you buy will taste fantastic and cost less. Look out for good deals at supermarkets, farm shops, markets and greengrocers where you can sometimes buy larger, cheaper quantities for freezing or batch cooking. Pick Your Own farms often charge half the price of the supermarkets. You can pick fruit and vegetables at their ripest and enjoy a fun day out with the family too.

	Vegetables	Fruit
JANUARY	Beetroot, Brussels sprouts, cauliflower, celeriac, celery, chicory, Jerusalem artichoke, kale, leeks, parsnips, potatoes (maincrop), rhubarb, swede, turnips	Apples, clementines, kiwi fruit, lemons, oranges, passion fruit, pears, pineapples, pomegranates, satsumas, tangerines, walnuts
FEBRUARY	Brussels sprouts, cauliflower, celeriac, chicory, kale, leeks, parsnips, potatoes (maincrop), rhubarb, swede	Bananas, blood oranges, kiwi fruit, lemons, oranges, passion fruit, pears, pineapples, pomegranates
MARCH	Cauliflower, chicory, kale, leeks, purple sprouting broccoli, rhubarb, spring onions	Bananas, blood oranges, kiwi fruit, lemons, oranges, passion fruit, pineapples, pomegranates
APRIL	Asparagus, broccoli, Jersey royal potatoes, purple sprouting broccoli, radishes, rhubarb, rocket, spinach, spring onions, watercress	Bananas, kiwi fruit
MAY	Asparagus, broccoli, Jersey royal potatoes, new potatoes, radishes, rhubarb, rocket, spinach, spring onions, watercress	Cherries, kiwi fruit, strawberries
JUNE	Artichokes, asparagus, aubergines, broad beans, broccoli, carrots, courgettes, fennel, mangetouts, Jersey royal potatoes, new potatoes, peas, radishes, rocket, runner beans, spring onions, turnips, watercress	Cherries, strawberries

	Vegetables	Fruit
JULY	Artichokes, aubergines, beetroot, broad beans, broccoli, carrots, courgettes, cucumber, fennel, French beans, garlic, mangetouts, new potatoes, onions, peas, potatoes (maincrop), radishes, rocket, runner beans, turnips, watercress	Apricots, blackberries, blueberries, cherries, gooseberries, greengages, kiwi fruit, melons, peaches, raspberries, redcurrants, strawberries, tomatoes
AUGUST	Artichokes, aubergines, beetroot, broad beans, broccoli, carrots, courgettes, cucumber, fennel, french beans, garlic, leeks, mangetout, marrow, new potatoes, onions, peas, peppers, potatoes (maincrop), radishes, rocket, runner beans, sweetcorn, watercress	Apricots, blackberries, blueberries, damsons, greengages, kiwi fruit, melons, nectarines, peaches, plums, raspberries, redcurrants, tomatoes
SEPTEMBER	Artichokes, aubergines, beetroot, broccoli, butternut squash, carrots, courgettes, cucumber, fennel, garlic, leeks, mangetouts, marrow, onions, parsnips, peas, peppers, potatoes (maincrop), radishes, rocket, runner beans, sweetcorn, watercress, wild mushrooms	Apples, blackberries, damsons, figs, grapes, melons, nectarines, peaches, pears, plums, raspberries, redcurrants, tomatoes, walnuts
OCTOBER	Artichokes, beetroot, broccoli, butternut squash, carrots, celeriac, celery, fennel, kale, leeks, marrow, onions, parsnips, potatoes (maincrop), pumpkin, swede, turnips, watercress, wild mushrooms	Apples, chestnuts, figs, pears, quince, tomatoes, walnuts
NOVEMBER	Artichokes, beetroot, Brussels sprouts, celeriac, celery, chicory, kale, leeks, parsnips, potatoes (maincrop), pumpkin, swede, turnips, watercress, wild mushrooms	Apples, chestnuts, clementines, cranberries, figs, passion fruit, pears, quince, satsumas, tangerines, walnuts
DECEMBER	Beetroot, Brussels sprouts, cauliflower, celeriac, celery, chicory, kale, leeks, parsnips, potatoes (maincrop), pumpkin, swede, turnips	Apples, chestnuts, clementines, cranberries, passion fruit, pears, pineapple, pomegranate, satsumas, tangerines, walnuts

Roasted Root Vegetable Salad

Hands-on time: 20 minutes
Cooking time: 40 minutes, plus cooling

1 butternut squash, halved, seeded and cubed
1½ large carrots, cut into chunks
3 fresh thyme sprigs
1½ tbsp olive oil
2 red onions, cut into wedges
1 tbsp balsamic vinegar
400g can chickpeas, drained and rinsed
25g (1oz) pinenuts, toasted
100g (3½oz) wild rocket
salt and freshly ground black pepper

1 Preheat the oven to 190°C (170°C fan oven) mark 5. Put the squash and carrots into a large deep roasting tin. Scatter the thyme sprigs over them, drizzle with 1 tbsp of the oil and season with salt and ground black pepper. Roast in the oven for 20 minutes.

2 Take the tin out of the oven, give it a good shake to make sure the vegetables aren't sticking, then add the onions. Drizzle the remaining oil over and toss to coat. Roast for a further 20 minutes or until all the vegetables are tender.

3 Remove the roasted vegetables from the oven and discard any twiggy sprigs of thyme. Drizzle the vinegar over, stir in and leave to cool.

4 To serve, put the chickpeas into a large serving bowl. Add the cooled vegetables, the pinenuts and rocket (putting a few leaves to one side). Toss everything together and garnish with the reserved rocket.

SAVE TIME

Complete the recipe to the end of step 3, then cool, cover and chill for up to two days. Complete step 4 to serve.

Serves 4

Perfect Griddling and Grilling

A few vegetables are perfect for cooking on a griddle or under the grill before being added to salads. Those that work well in both methods are courgettes and aubergines. Peppers (whole or halved) can be grilled and so can fennel, onions and sweet potatoes, with careful slicing.

Lemon and Dill Courgettes

To serve four, you will need: 450g (1lb) courgettes, cut lengthways into 5mm (¼in) slices, or quartered if small, about 6 tbsp extra virgin olive oil, ½ lemon, a small handful of fresh dill.

1 Preheat the griddle over a medium-high heat. Brush the courgettes with oil.
2 Cook the courgettes without disturbing them until they have deep brown seared lines underneath – about 2–3 minutes. Turn them and griddle until seared underneath and tender, but still with a hint of bite.
3 Transfer to a plate, squeeze lemon juice over tand scatter with dill.

Perfect griddling

- Vegetables have a lovely flavour when cooked on the griddle, as well as attractive browned lines if you use a ridged griddle.
- The choice of vegetable is crucial in griddling: you have to use something that has a fairly even surface so that it will lie flat on the griddle and won't break up when it's turned.

- Don't slice the vegetables too thickly or they will burn before they are fully cooked – 1cm (½in) should be the maximum thickness.
- Lay the vegetables on a board and brush them with oil so that it coats them thoroughly.
- Cook over a medium-high heat and turn once, when they have browned underneath.

3

Grilled Avocado, Tomato and Mozzarella Salad

Hands-on time: 20 minutes, plus standing
Cooking time: about 10 minutes

1kg (2lb 2oz) mixed tomatoes
2 ripe avocados, but not overly soft
1 tbsp extra virgin olive oil, plus extra
   to drizzle
2 × 125g (4oz) balls buffalo mozzarella,
   drained
a punnet of cress or a large handful of
   Greek basil
balsamic vinegar to drizzle
salt and freshly ground black pepper
crusty bread to serve

1 Start by preparing the tomatoes. To add interest to your salad, chop all the tomatoes differently – halve or quarter smaller ones, slice or roughly chop larger ones. Put all the tomatoes into a colander and sprinkle with ½ tsp salt, then toss together and leave in the sink for 20 minutes – this will help any excess, flavourless moisture drain out of the tomatoes.

2 Meanwhile, halve, stone and peel the avocados. Slice the flesh into 1cm (½in) thick slices. Preheat a griddle pan over a high heat. Brush the avocado slices with the oil and arrange neatly on the griddle. Leave in place until charred black lines appear on the underside of the slices, then flip over and repeat on the other side.

3 To serve, tip the tomatoes on to a large flat platter. Rip the mozzarella into bite-size pieces and dot among the tomatoes. Snip the cress over or sprinkle with basil. Season with ground black pepper and drizzle with some balsamic vinegar and extra virgin olive oil. Serve with crusty bread.

Serves 4

Perfect Grains

Grains such as wheat, barley and quinoa are the edible seeds of different grasses. Many of these grains are available in a variety of forms; as side dishes they make good low-GI alternatives to rice and potatoes.

Quinoa

Originally from South America, quinoa is packed with protein and absorbs flavours easily. It makes a great alternative to rice.

1. Put the quinoa in a bowl of cold water and mix well. Soak for 2 minutes, then drain.
2. Put the quinoa into a pan with twice its volume of water. Bring to the boil, then reduce the heat and simmer for 20 minutes. Take off the heat, cover and leave to stand for 10 minutes. To use in salads, drain and run it under cold water to cool it quickly.

Pearl barley

Barley comes in several forms, so you should check which type you have bought.

Pearl barley has had its outer husk removed and needs no soaking. Rinse the barley in cold water, then put it into a pan with twice its volume of water. Bring to the boil, then reduce the heat and simmer until tender – 25–30 minutes. To use in salads, drain and run it under cold water to cool it quickly.

Bulgur wheat

A form of cracked wheat, bulgur has had some or all of the bran removed. It is good served as an accompaniment or used in salads. It is pre-boiled during manufacturing, and may be boiled, steamed or soaked.

Simmering bulgur

Put the bulgur into a pan and add water to cover by about 2.5cm (1in). Bring to the boil, then reduce the heat and simmer for 10–15 minutes until just tender. Drain well.

Steaming bulgur

Place the bulgur in a steamer lined with a clean teatowel and steam over boiling water for 20 minutes or until the grains are soft.

Soaking bulgur

Put the bulgur into a deep bowl. Cover with hot water and mix with a fork. Leave to steep for 20 minutes, checking to make sure there is enough water. Drain and fluff up with a fork.

Quantities

Allow 50–75g (2–3oz) raw grain per person. Or, if measuring by volume, allow 50–75ml (2–2½fl oz).

Beetroot and Bulgur Wheat Salad

Hands-on time: 15 minutes
Cooking time: about 30 minutes

2 red onions, each cut into eight wedges

2 medium beetroot (total weight about 300g/11oz), peeled and cut into wedges

1 tbsp olive oil, plus extra to drizzle

200g (7oz) bulgur wheat

350ml (12fl oz) vegetable or chicken stock

200g (7oz) frozen soya beans or peas

juice of 1 lemon

100g (3½oz) feta cheese, crumbled

a large handful of fresh mint, roughly chopped

100g (3½oz) spinach leaves

salt and freshly ground black pepper

1 Preheat the oven to 200°C (180°C fan oven) mark 6. Put the onions and beetroot wedges on a baking tray, add the oil, then season well and gently toss together. Roast for 25–30 minutes until tender.

2 Meanwhile, toast the bulgur wheat in a medium pan over a medium heat for 2 minutes to bring out its nutty flavour. Carefully pour in the stock (it will bubble wildly). Simmer for 5 minutes, then add the soya beans or peas and continue cooking for 3 minutes. Leave for 10 minutes to cool slightly, then fork through the mixture to loosen and fluff it up. Stir in the lemon juice, feta, mint and spinach leaves and check the seasoning.

3 Divide the bulgur mixture among four serving plates. Top each with some of the roasted vegetables and drizzle some extra oil over, if you like.

Serves 4

Gluten-free Quinoa and Halloumi Salad

Hands-on time: 15 minutes
Cooking time: about 25 minutes

200g (7oz) quinoa
150g (5oz) fresh or frozen peas
250g pack of halloumi
2 tbsp rapeseed oil, plus extra to brush
3 spring onions, finely sliced
70g bag rocket
finely grated zest and juice of 1 lemon
a small handful each of fresh mint and
   parsley, roughly chopped
salt and freshly ground black pepper

1 Put the quinoa into a large pan and cover well with water. Bring to the boil, then reduce the heat and simmer until tender – about 20 minutes. Add the fresh or frozen peas to the pan for the final 2 minutes of cooking.

2 Meanwhile, preheat a griddle pan over a high heat. Cut the halloumi into 5mm (¼in) thick slices and brush both sides with oil. Grill for 4 minutes, turning once, or until the cheese has charred lines on both sides and has softened. Transfer to a board and leave to cool.

3 Put the spring onions and rocket into a large serving bowl. Put the oil, lemon zest and juice and plenty of seasoning into a small jug and mix well. Put to one side.

4 Drain the cooked quinoa mixture and run it under cold water to cool it quickly. Drain well and add to the serving bowl. Rip the halloumi into bite-size pieces and add to the bowl, together with the herbs and dressing. Toss everything together and check the seasoning before serving.

Serves 4

Fresh and Fruity Barley Salad

Hands-on time: 15 minutes
Cooking time: about 30 minutes

250g (9oz) pearl barley

125g (4oz) tenderstem broccoli, trimmed

2 peaches

½ cucumber, halved lengthways, seeded and diced

a small handful of fresh mint, roughly chopped

50g (2oz) rocket

410g can chickpeas, drained and rinsed

2 tbsp balsamic vinegar

1 tbsp extra virgin olive oil

salt and freshly ground black pepper

1 Put the pearl barley into a large pan and cover well with water. Add some salt and bring to the boil, then reduce the heat and simmer for about 25 minutes until the barley is just tender. Add the broccoli for the final 3 minutes of cooking. Drain and put to one side.

2 Meanwhile, peel and halve the peaches and discard the stones. Cut each peach half into four wedges, then put the wedges into a large serving bowl. Add the cucumber, mint, rocket and chickpeas.

3 Add the vinegar, oil and some seasoning to the peach bowl, then add the drained barley mixture and lightly mix through. Check the seasoning and serve.

Serves 4

Couscous and Haddock Salad

Hands-on time: 15 minutes
Cooking time: about 10 minutes

175g (6oz) couscous

125g (4oz) cooked smoked haddock, flaked

50g (2oz) cooked peas

a pinch of curry powder

2 spring onions, sliced

1 tbsp freshly chopped flat-leafed parsley

1 small hard-boiled egg, chopped

2 tbsp olive oil

2 tsp lemon juice

salt and freshly ground black pepper

1 Cook the couscous according to the pack instructions. Drain if necessary.

2 Mix the couscous with the smoked haddock, peas, curry powder, spring onions, parsley and egg.

3 Toss with the oil, lemon juice and plenty of salt and ground black pepper to taste, then serve.

Serves 4

Perfect Eggs

Follow these tried and tested steps for perfect poached, coddled and boiled eggs.

Perfect poaching

1 Heat about 8cm (3¼in) of lightly salted water in a shallow frying pan to a bare simmer. Crack a very fresh egg into a cup, then slip it into the water. (The whites in a fresh egg are firmer and will form a 'nest' for the yolk, while older egg whites are watery and spread out in the pan.)
2 Cook for 3–4 minutes until the white is barely set. Remove the egg with a slotted spoon and drain on kitchen paper.

Perfect coddling

1 Using a slotted spoon, gently lower the whole eggs into a pan of simmering water, then take the pan off the heat.
2 Leave the eggs to stand in the water for 4–5 minutes, where they will cook gently with the residual heat of the water.

Perfect boiling

Boiling: method 1
1. Bring a small pan of water to the boil. Once the water is boiling, add a medium egg. For a soft-boiled egg, cook for 6 minutes; for a salad egg, cook for 8 minutes; for a hard-boiled egg, cook for 10 minutes.
2. Remove the egg from the water with a slotted spoon and serve.

Boiling: method 2
1. Put a medium egg into a small pan and cover with cold water. Put on a lid and bring to the boil. When the water begins to boil, take off the lid and cook for 2 minutes for a soft-boiled egg, 5 minutes for a salad egg, and 7 minutes for a hard-boiled egg.
2. Remove the egg from the water with a slotted spoon and serve.

Eggs Florentine Salad

Hands-on time: 15 minutes
Cooking time: 15 minutes

5 medium whole eggs, plus 2 medium
  egg yolks

75g (3oz) unsalted butter

90g pack of sliced Parma ham

2 English muffins, cut into 1cm
  (½in) cubes

½ tsp prepared English mustard

½ tbsp white wine vinegar

2 tbsp freshly chopped tarragon

225g (8oz) mix of baby spinach
  and rocket

salt and freshly ground black pepper

1 Bring a small pan of water to the
boil. Add the whole eggs and
simmer for 5 minutes. Drain, then
run the eggs under cold water for
1 minute. Shell and put to one side.

2 Heat 1 tbsp of the butter in a large
frying pan. Add the Parma ham
and fry for 2 minutes, turning once,
or until golden and crisp. Drain on
kitchen paper.

3 In the same pan, fry the muffin
cubes until golden and crisp. Leave

to drain on kitchen paper. Thickly
slice the Parma ham and cut the
eggs into quarters.

4 Put the raw egg yolks into a blender
with the mustard and vinegar.
Season well with salt and ground
black pepper. Melt the remaining
butter in a small pan. With the
motor of the blender running,
gradually pour in the melted butter
(the mixture will thicken). Empty
into a bowl and stir in the tarragon.

5 Divide the spinach and rocket,
the eggs, Parma ham and muffin
croûtons among four plates, then
spoon the dressing over. Serve
immediately.

Note: As this dressing contains raw
eggs, buy those with the British Lion
mark and don't serve to vulnerable
groups.

Serves 4

Warm Lentil Salad

Hands-on time: 10 minutes
Cooking time: about 10 minutes

2 medium eggs
2 tsp olive oil
2 small leeks, trimmed and chopped
4 spring onions, chopped
1 red pepper, seeded and chopped
400g can lentils, drained
150ml (¼ pint) vegetable stock
a handful of rocket
salt and freshly ground black pepper

1 Bring a small pan of water to the boil. Gently lower the eggs into the pan, reduce the heat and simmer for 7 minutes.

2 Meanwhile, heat the oil in a separate pan and fry the leeks, spring onions and red pepper for 6–8 minutes until softened.

3 Stir in the lentils and stock and bring to the boil, then reduce the heat and simmer for 1–2 minutes.

4 Shell the eggs, then cut in half. Season the lentil mixture with salt and ground black pepper, then divide between two serving bowls and top each with an egg and a few rocket leaves.

Serves 2

Asparagus and Quail Egg Salad

Hands-on time: 30 minutes
Cooking time: 4 minutes, plus cooling

24 quail eggs
24 asparagus spears, trimmed
juice of ½ lemon
5 tbsp olive oil
4 large spring onions, finely sliced
100g (3½oz) watercress, roughly
  chopped
a few fresh dill and tarragon sprigs
salt and freshly ground black pepper

1 Gently lower the quail eggs into a pan of boiling water and cook for 2 minutes, then drain and plunge them into cold water. Cook the asparagus in salted boiling water for 2 minutes or until just tender. Drain, plunge into cold water and leave to cool.

2 Whisk together the lemon juice and oil and season with salt and ground black pepper. Stir in the spring onions and put to one side.

3 Shell the quail eggs and cut in half. Put into a large bowl with the asparagus, watercress, dill and tarragon. Pour the dressing over and lightly toss all the ingredients together. Adjust the seasoning and serve immediately.

Serves 8

Provençale Tuna and Pepper Salad

Hands-on time: 15 minutes
Cooking time: about 15 minutes

400g (14oz) new potatoes, halved if large
200g (7oz) green beans
4 medium eggs
1 tbsp extra virgin olive oil
grated zest and juice of 1 lemon
50g (2oz) black olives, pitted
300g (11oz) ready-roasted red peppers, cut into thick strips
185g can tuna chunks, drained
25g pack of fresh basil leaves, torn
salt and freshly ground black pepper

1 Bring a medium pan of water to the boil. Add the potatoes, reduce the heat and simmer for 10 minutes or until tender, adding the beans for the final 4 minutes of cooking. Drain and leave to steam-dry until needed.

2 Meanwhile, bring a small pan of water to the boil, add the eggs, reduce the heat and simmer for 8 minutes. Drain and run them under cold water. Shell and quarter the eggs, then put them to one side. Put the oil, lemon zest and juice with seasoning to taste into a small bowl and whisk to combine.

3 Put the potatoes, green beans, olives, pepper strips, tuna and basil leaves into a large serving dish. Add the dressing and gently toss through (using your hands is best). Garnish with the egg quarters and serve immediately.

102

4 Classic Salad Dressings

Basic Vinaigrette

To make about 300ml (½ pint), you will need:

100ml (3½fl oz) extra virgin olive oil, 100ml (3½fl oz) grapeseed oil, 50ml (2fl oz) white wine vinegar, a pinch each of sugar and English mustard powder, 1 crushed garlic clove (optional), salt and freshly ground black pepper.

1 Put both oils, the vinegar, sugar, mustard powder and garlic, if you like, into a large screw-topped jar. Tighten the lid and shake well. Season to taste with salt and ground black pepper.
2 If not using immediately, store in a cool place and shake briefly before using.

Balsamic Dressing

To make about 100ml (3½fl oz), you will need:

2 tbsp balsamic vinegar, 4 tbsp extra virgin olive oil, salt and freshly ground black pepper.

1 Whisk the vinegar and oil in a small bowl. Season with salt and ground black pepper to taste.
2 If not using immediately, store in a cool place and whisk briefly before using.

SAVE EFFORT

To help it emulsify easily, add 1 tsp cold water to the dressing. To get a really good emulsion, shake the dressing vigorously in a screw-topped jar.

French Dressing

To make 100ml (3½fl oz), you will need:
1 tsp Dijon mustard, a pinch of
sugar, 1 tbsp red or white wine
vinegar, 6 tbsp extra virgin
olive oil, salt and freshly ground
black pepper.

1 Put the mustard, sugar and
   vinegar into a small bowl and
   season with salt and ground
   black pepper. Whisk thoroughly
   until well combined, then
   gradually whisk in the oil until
   thoroughly combined.
2 If not using immediately, store
   in a cool place and whisk briefly
   before using.

French Dressing variations

Herb Dressing Use half the
mustard, replace the vinegar with
lemon juice, and add 2 tbsp freshly
chopped herbs, such as parsley,
chervil and chives.

Garlic Dressing Add 1 crushed
garlic clove to the dressing in step 2.

Caesar Dressing

To make about 150ml (¼ pint), you
will need:
1 medium egg, 1 garlic clove, juice
of ½ lemon, 2 tsp Dijon mustard,
1 tsp balsamic vinegar, 150ml
(¼ pint) sunflower oil, salt and
freshly ground black pepper.

1 Put the egg, garlic, lemon juice,
   mustard and vinegar into a food
   processor and whiz until smooth,
   then, with the motor running,
   gradually add the oil and whiz
   until smooth. Season with salt
   and ground black pepper.
2 If not using immediately, cover
   and chill for up to three days.
   Whisk briefly before using.

Note: As this dressing contains raw
eggs, buy those with the British Lion
mark and don't serve to vulnerable
groups.

Chicken Caesar Salad

Hands-on time: about 20 minutes
Cooking time: 12 minutes

2 tbsp olive oil
1 garlic clove, crushed
2 thick slices country-style bread, cubed
6 tbsp freshly grated Parmesan
1 cos lettuce, washed, chilled and cut into bite-size pieces
700g (1½lb) cooked chicken breast, sliced

For the dressing
4 tbsp mayonnaise
2 tbsp lemon juice
1 tsp Dijon mustard
2 anchovy fillets, very finely chopped
salt and freshly ground black pepper

1 Preheat the oven to 180°C (160°C fan oven) mark 4. Put the oil, garlic and bread cubes into a bowl and toss well. Tip on to a baking sheet and bake in the oven for 10 minutes, turning halfway through.
2 Sprinkle the Parmesan over the croûtons and bake for 2 minutes or until the cheese has melted and the bread is golden.
3 Whisk all the dressing ingredients together in a small bowl with some seasoning.
4 Put the lettuce and sliced chicken into a bowl, pour the dressing over and toss to combine. Top with the cheese croûtons.

Serves 4

Chicken Salad

Hands-on time: 15 minutes
Cooking time: about 10 minutes

40g (1½oz) pinenuts
500g (1lb 2oz) asparagus, woody ends trimmed
2 × 70g bags rocket
4 skinless ready-cooked chicken breasts, ripped into bite-size pieces
100g (3½oz) goat's cheese, crumbled
bread to serve

For the dressing

2 tbsp runny honey
1 tbsp wholegrain mustard
1 tbsp white wine vinegar
2 tbsp extra virgin olive oil
salt and freshly ground black pepper

1 Heat a pan over a medium heat and add the pinenuts. Toast until golden (watch them carefully, as they burn quickly). Empty on to a plate and put to one side. Half-fill the pan with water and bring to the boil.

2 Meanwhile, roughly chop each asparagus spear into two or three pieces. Cook the asparagus pieces in the boiling water for 2–3 minutes until just tender, then drain and run them under cold water for 15 seconds to cool down and set the green colour.

3 Whisk all the dressing ingredients together in a small bowl with some seasoning.

4 Put the rocket, chicken, pinenuts, asparagus, goat's cheese and dressing into a large bowl and toss together. Serve with bread.

SAVE EFFORT

This salad would also make a tasty starter for six.

Serves 4

Perfect Pasta

There are a number of mistaken ideas about cooking pasta, such as adding oil to the water, adding salt only at a certain point and rinsing the pasta after cooking. The basics couldn't be simpler. Filled pasta is the only type of pasta that needs oil in the cooking water – the oil reduces friction, which could tear the wrappers and allow the filling to come out. Use 1 tbsp for a large pan of water. Rinse pasta after cooking only if you are going to cool it to use in a salad.

Whether you are cooking dried or fresh pasta, follow these simple steps.

Dried pasta

1 Heat the water with about 1 tsp salt per 100g (3½oz) of pasta. Bring to a rolling boil, then add all the pasta and stir well for 30 seconds, to keep the pasta from sticking.

2 Once the water is boiling again, set the timer for 2 minutes less than the cooking time on the pack and cook uncovered.

3 Check the pasta when the timer goes off, then every 60 seconds until it is cooked al dente: tender, but with a little bite at the centre. Drain in a colander. The pasta will continue to cook a little after draining.

Fresh pasta
Fresh pasta is cooked in the same way as dried, but for a shorter time. Bring the water to the boil. Add the pasta to the boiling water all at once and stir well. Set the timer for 2 minutes and keep testing every 30 seconds until the pasta is cooked al dente: tender, but with a little bite at the centre. Drain in a colander. The pasta will continue to cook a little after draining.

How much pasta do I need?
Allow 75g (3oz) dried pasta shapes or noodles or 125g (4oz) fresh or filled pasta shapes per person.

2

Pasta, Salami and Tapenade Salad

Hands-on time: 5 minutes

3 × 225g tubs pasta salad in
tomato sauce
75g (3oz) pepper salami, shredded
3 tbsp black olive tapenade paste
3 tbsp freshly chopped chives
salt and freshly ground black pepper

1 Turn the pasta salad into a large bowl, add the salami, tapenade and chives. Toss everything together and season with ground black pepper. Check for seasoning before adding salt – the tapenade may have made the salad salty enough.

2 Pile the salad into a large serving bowl. If not being served straight away, this salad is best kept in a cool place, but not chilled, until needed.

Serves 4

Greek Pasta Salad

Hands-on time: 10 minutes
Cooking time: 20 minutes

3 tbsp olive oil
2 tbsp lemon juice
150g (5oz) cooked pasta shapes,
  cooled
75g (3oz) feta, crumbled
3 tomatoes, roughly chopped
2 tbsp small pitted black olives
½ cucumber, roughly chopped
1 small red onion, finely sliced
salt and freshly ground black pepper
freshly chopped parsley and lemon
  zest to garnish
crusty bread to serve

1 Mix the oil and lemon juice together
  in a salad bowl, then add the pasta,
  feta, tomatoes, olives, cucumber
  and onion. Season to taste with
  salt and ground black pepper, then
  stir to mix.
2 Garnish with parsley and lemon zest
  and serve with crusty bread.

Serves 2

Warm Bacon Salad

Hands-on time: 10 minutes
Cooking time: about 15 minutes

4 handfuls of soft salad leaves
1 small red onion, thinly sliced
75g (3oz) cubed pancetta
1 thick slice white bread, diced
2 medium eggs
25g (1oz) Parmesan, pared into
   shavings with a vegetable peeler
fresh flat-leafed parsley sprigs
   to garnish

For the dressing

1 tbsp Dijon mustard
2 tbsp red wine vinegar
2 tbsp fruity olive oil
salt and freshly ground black pepper

1 Put the salad leaves and onion into a large bowl. Fry the pancetta in a non-stick frying pan until it begins to release some fat. Add the diced bread and continue to fry until the pancetta is golden and crisp.

2 Whisk all the dressing ingredients together in a small bowl with some seasoning.

3 Half-fill a small pan with cold water and bring to the boil. Turn the heat right down – there should be just a few bubbles on the bottom of the pan. Break the eggs into a cup, then tip them gently into the pan and cook for 3–4 minutes, using a metal spoon to baste the tops with a little of the hot water. Lift the eggs out of the water with a slotted spoon and drain on kitchen paper.

4 Tip the pancetta, bread and any pan juices over the salad leaves. Add the Parmesan, then pour the dressing over the salad. Toss well, then divide between two plates. Top each with an egg, season to taste, then garnish with parsley sprigs and serve.

Serves 2

Spicy Salads

Vietnamese Rice Salad

Hands-on time: 10 minutes
Cooking time: about 25 minutes, plus cooling

225g (8oz) mixed basmati and wild rice
1 large carrot, coarsely grated
1 large courgette, coarsely grated
1 red onion, finely sliced
4 tbsp roasted salted peanuts,
    lightly chopped
20g (¾oz) each fresh coriander, mint
    and basil, roughly chopped
100g (3½oz) wild rocket

For the Vietnamese dressing

2 tbsp light muscovado sugar
juice of 2 limes
4 tbsp fish sauce
6 tbsp rice wine vinegar or white
    wine vinegar
2 tbsp sunflower oil

1 Put the rice into a pan with 500ml
(18fl oz) water. Cover and bring to
the boil, then reduce the heat and
cook for 20 minutes or until the rice
is just cooked. Tip on to a plastic
tray, spread out and leave to cool.

2 Meanwhile, make the dressing. Put
the sugar into a small pan and heat
gently until it just begins to dissolve.
Add the lime juice, fish sauce and
vinegar and stir over a low heat to
dissolve the sugar. Take off the heat
and add the oil. Stir into the rice
with the grated carrot, courgette and
sliced onion.

3 Spoon the salad into a large bowl
and top with peanuts, herbs and
rocket. Cover and keep chilled until
ready to serve.

SAVE TIME

Complete the recipe up to the
end of step 2 and store in an
airtight container in the fridge for
up to two days. Complete step 3
to finish the recipe.

Serves 6

Thai Noodle Salad

Hands-on time: 20 minutes, plus soaking
Cooking time: about 8 minutes

200g (7oz) sugarsnap peas, trimmed
250g pack of Thai stir-fry rice noodles
100g (3½oz) cashew nuts
300g (11oz) carrots, cut into batons
10 spring onions, sliced on the
   diagonal
300g (11oz) bean sprouts
20g (¾oz) fresh coriander, roughly
   chopped, plus fresh coriander sprigs
   to garnish
1 red bird's eye chilli, seeded and
   finely chopped (see Safety Tip,
   page 142)
2 tsp sweet chilli sauce
4 tbsp sesame oil
6 tbsp soy sauce
juice of 2 limes
salt and freshly ground black pepper

1 Bring a pan of salted water to the boil and blanch the sugarsnap peas for 2–3 minutes until just tender to the bite. Drain and refresh under cold water.

2 Put the noodles into a bowl, cover with boiling water and leave to soak for 4 minutes. Rinse under cold water and drain very well.

3 Toast the cashews in a dry frying pan until golden – about 5 minutes.

4 Put the sugarsnaps into a large glass serving bowl. Add the carrots, spring onions, bean sprouts, chopped coriander, chopped chilli, cashews and noodles.

5 Mix the chilli sauce with the sesame oil, soy sauce and lime juice and season well with salt and ground black pepper. Pour over the salad and toss together, then garnish with coriander sprigs and serve.

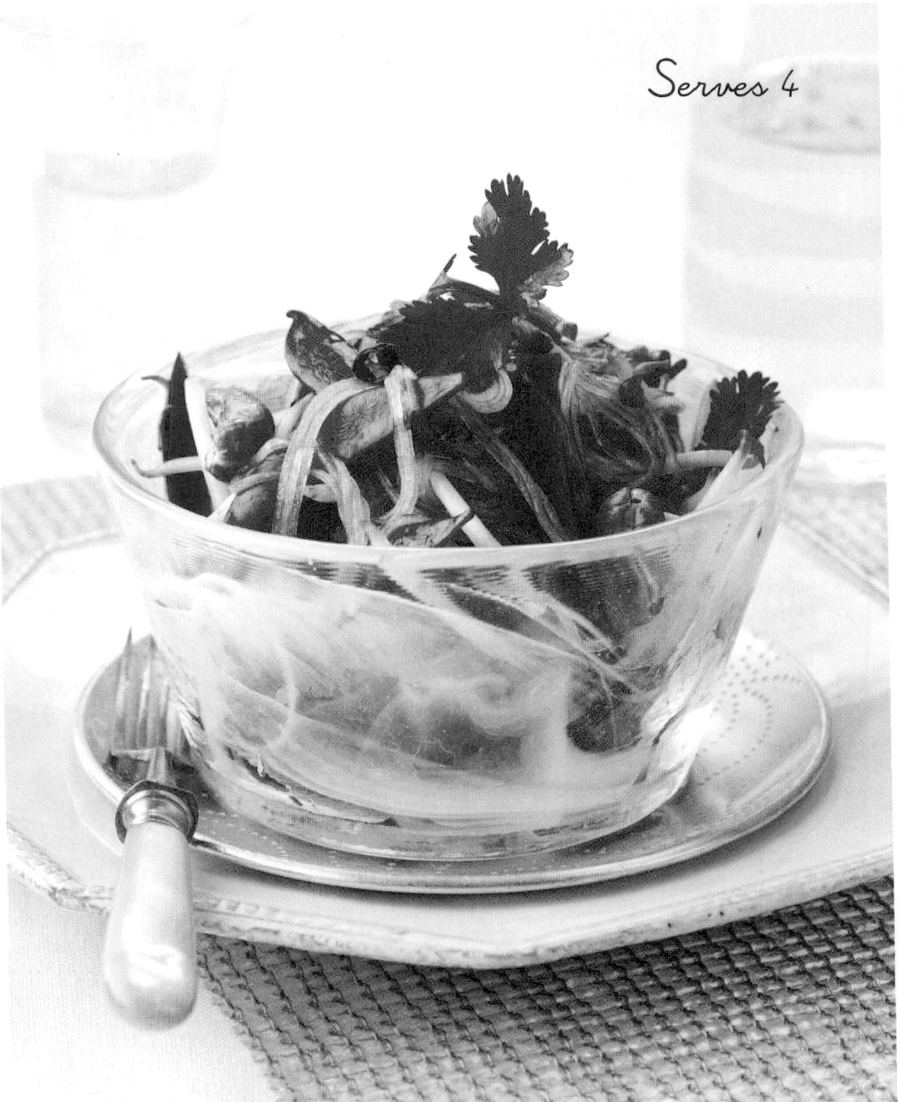
Serves 4

Warm Spiced Salmon Niçoise

Hands-on time: 15 minutes
Cooking time: 15 minutes

350g (12oz) new potatoes,
   thickly sliced
175g (6oz) fine green beans, halved
175g (6oz) cherry tomatoes, halved
1 small red onion, cut into thin wedges
4 × 150–175g (5–6oz) salmon fillets,
   skinned
15g (½oz) butter, melted
1 tbsp coriander seeds, crushed
½ tsp dried crushed chillies
4 tbsp Caesar Dressing (see page 105)
flaked sea salt and freshly ground
   black pepper
fresh chives to garnish

1 Cook the potatoes in salted boiling
   water for 8–10 minutes until just
   tender, adding the beans for the final
   2 minutes of cooking. Drain well,
   then transfer to a bowl and add the
   tomatoes and onion wedges.

2 Preheat the grill. Cut each salmon
   fillet into three strips. Place the
   strips in four piles on a baking sheet
   and brush each pile with the melted

butter. Mix the crushed coriander
seeds with the chillies and a little
sea salt and sprinkle evenly over
the salmon. Place under the hot grill
and cook for 4–5 minutes until just
cooked through.

3 Add 1 tbsp water to the Caesar
   Dressing to thin it slightly (it should
   be the consistency of single cream).
   Spoon three-quarters of the dressing
   over the vegetables and toss to coat.
   Season well.

4 Divide the vegetables among four
   serving plates, top with the salmon
   pieces and drizzle the remaining
   dressing around the edge of the
   salad. Garnish with chives and
   serve immediately.

SAVE EFFORT

An easy way to get a brand new
dish is to use another firm fish,
such as sea bass or monkfish.

Serves 4

Perfect Herbs

Most herbs are the leaf of a flowering plant and are usually sold with much of the stalk intact. They have to be washed, trimmed and then chopped or torn into pieces suitable for your recipe.

Washing

1 Trim the roots and part of the stalks from the herbs. Immerse in cold water and shake briskly. Leave in the water for a few minutes.
2 Lift out of the water and put into a colander or sieve, then rinse again under cold water. Leave to drain for a few minutes, then dry thoroughly on kitchen paper or teatowels, or use a salad spinner.

SAVE EFFORT

- Don't pour the herbs and their water into the sieve, because dirt in the water might get caught in the leaves.
- If the herb has fleshy stalks, such as parsley or coriander, the stalks can be saved to flavour stock or soup. Tie them in a bundle with kitchen string for easy removal.

Chopping

1 Trim the herbs by pinching off all but the smallest, most tender stalks. If the herb is one with a woody stalk, such as rosemary or thyme, it may be easier to remove the leaves by rubbing the whole bunch between your hands; the leaves should simply pull off the stems.

2 If you are chopping the leaves, gather them into a compact ball in one hand, keeping your fist around the ball (but being careful not to crush them).

3 Chop with a large knife, using a rocking motion and letting just a little of the ball out of your fingers at a time.

4 When the herbs are roughly chopped, continue chopping until the pieces are in small shreds or flakes.

Chinese Prawn Noodle Salad

Hands-on time: 15 minutes, plus soaking and chilling

450g (1lb) straight-to-wok medium egg
  noodles
2 red chillies, seeded and finely
  chopped (see Safety Tip, page 142)
4 spring onions, finely sliced
½ cucumber, halved lengthways,
  seeded and finely diced
350g (12oz) cooked prawns
1 tbsp freshly chopped coriander

For the soy and sesame dressing

2 tbsp runny honey
2 tbsp dark soy sauce
2 tbsp rice wine vinegar
4 tbsp sesame oil
freshly ground black pepper

1 Put the noodles into a bowl and pour
boiling water over them to cover.
Cover with clingfilm and leave for
5 minutes.

2 To make the dressing, whisk the
honey, soy sauce, vinegar and
sesame oil together with some
ground black pepper. Drain the
noodles and, while they are still
warm, pour the dressing over them.
Toss together, then leave to cool.

3 To serve, stir the chillies, spring
onions, cucumber, prawns and
coriander into the noodles and pile
into four bowls. If you have time,
chill for 30 minutes–1 hour.

Serves 4

King Prawn Thai-style Salad

Hands-on time: 10 minutes
Cooking time: 5 minutes

2–3 tbsp green curry paste
200g (7oz) raw king prawns, peeled and deveined
juice of ½ lime
2 large carrots, peeled into ribbons
1 cucumber, peeled into ribbons
100g (3½oz) fresh coconut, cubed (see Save Effort)
a small handful of fresh mint, chopped
salt and freshly ground black pepper
lime wedges to serve

1 Heat a large frying pan, then stir in the curry paste and 1–2 tbsp hot water to loosen the paste. Cook for 30 seconds. Add the prawns and cook for 2–3 minutes until pink and cooked through.

2 Turn into a serving dish, then add the lime juice, carrots, cucumber, coconut and mint and toss to combine. Check the seasoning and serve with lime wedges to squeeze over.

SAVE EFFORT

Many supermarkets sell packs of fresh coconut in the chilled fruit section.

Harissa Chicken and Couscous Salad

Hands-on time: 15 minutes
Cooking time: about 25 minutes

1 tbsp rose harissa paste
4 skinless chicken breasts
1 litre (1¾ pints) chicken stock
200g (7oz) giant wholewheat couscous
½ courgette, finely chopped
100g (3½oz) cherry tomatoes, quartered
2 spring onions, finely sliced
40g (1½oz) feta, crumbled
a large handful of fresh coriander leaves, roughly chopped
salt and freshly ground black pepper
tzatziki to serve (optional)

1 Preheat the oven to 200°C (180°C fan oven) mark 6. Rub the harissa paste over the chicken breasts and put them on a baking tray. Roast for 20–25 minutes until cooked through.

2 Meanwhile, bring the stock to the boil in a large pan. Add the couscous and simmer according to the pack instructions or until tender – about 8 minutes. Drain.

3 Transfer the couscous to a large platter, add the courgette, tomatoes, onions, feta, coriander and some seasoning and mix through.

4 Carefully slice the cooked chicken and lay on top of the couscous salad. Serve warm or at room temperature, with tzatziki, if you like.

HEALTHY TIP

The tomatoes are full of vitamin C, which is a powerful antioxidant and antiviral nutrient crucial for a healthy immune system.

Serves 4

Take 5 Quick and Easy Salsas

Quick Tomato

Put 4 roughly chopped tomatoes, ½ ripe, peeled and roughly chopped avocado, 1 tsp olive oil and the juice of ½ lime into a bowl and stir well.

Smoky

Put 75g (3oz) finely chopped onions or shallots, 150ml (¼ pint) shop-bought barbecue sauce, 100ml (3½fl oz) maple syrup, 1 tbsp cider vinegar, 1 tbsp soft brown sugar, 100ml (3½fl oz) water, 1 tsp lemon juice and a little grated lemon zest into a pan. Bring to the boil and leave to bubble for 10–15 minutes until syrupy. Take the pan off the heat and add 6 finely chopped spring onions and 175g (6oz) finely chopped fresh pineapple. Serve warm or cold.

Mango and Fennel

Put 1 halved and diced mango, 1 small trimmed and diced fennel bulb, 1 seeded and finely diced chilli (see Safety Tip, page 142), 1 tbsp balsamic vinegar, 2 tbsp freshly chopped flat-leafed parsley and 2 tbsp freshly chopped mint into a bowl. Add the juice of 1 lime, stir to combine and season generously with salt and freshly ground black pepper.

Avocado, Tomato and Coriander

Put 1 chopped red onion into a bowl and add 1 ripe, peeled and chopped avocado, 4 large roughly chopped tomatoes, a small handful of roughly chopped fresh coriander and the juice of 1 lime. Mix well, then season with salt and freshly ground black pepper. Use at once.

Prawn and Avocado

Put 2 large ripe, peeled and roughly chopped avocados into a large bowl, then add 350g (12oz) cooked, peeled and deveined king prawns, 6 small finely sliced spring onions, 3 tbsp freshly chopped coriander, the grated zest and juice of 3 limes and 8 tbsp olive oil. Mix well, then season with salt and freshly ground black pepper. Use at once.

Skewered Chicken Salad with Sweet Chilli Sauce

Hands-on time: 15 minutes, plus soaking
Cooking time: 10 minutes

4 boneless, skinless chicken breasts, each cut into four strips

1 tbsp Cajun seasoning

2 tbsp groundnut oil, plus extra to grease

salt and freshly ground black pepper

For the salad

175g (6oz) small young carrots, cut into thin matchsticks

125g (4oz) cucumber, halved lengthways, seeded and cut into matchsticks

6 spring onions, cut into matchsticks

10 radishes, sliced

50g (2oz) bean sprouts, rinsed and dried

50g (2oz) unsalted peanuts, roughly chopped

1 large red chilli, seeded and finely chopped (see Safety Tip, page 142)

2 tsp sesame oil

Thai chilli dipping sauce to drizzle

1 Soak eight bamboo skewers in water for 20 minutes. Preheat the grill. Toss the chicken strips in the Cajun seasoning, then season with salt and ground black pepper and brush with oil. Thread on to the skewers.

2 Place the skewered chicken fillets on an oiled baking sheet and cook under the hot grill for 3–4 minutes on each side until cooked through.

3 Place all the salad vegetables, peanuts and chopped chilli in a bowl, toss with the sesame oil and season well with salt and pepper.

4 Divide the vegetables among four serving plates, top with the warm chicken skewers and drizzle with the chilli sauce. Serve immediately.

Serves 4

Mexican Chicken Salad

Hands-on time: 15 minutes

2 skinless ready-cooked chicken
   breasts
2 fresh corn on the cobs, or 225g (8oz)
   corn kernels
125g (4oz) mature Cheddar,
   coarsely grated
25g (1oz) jalapeño peppers, chopped
400g can kidney beans, drained
   and rinsed
½ red onion, very thinly sliced
¼–½ iceberg lettuce, thinly shredded,
   to taste
50g (2oz) soured cream
juice of 1 lime
50g (2oz) corn tortilla chips, crushed
salt and freshly ground black pepper

1 Rip or cut the chicken into bite-size pieces and put into a large mixing bowl. To slice the kernels off a corn cob, hold the cob upright (on its end) on a board and, using a large knife, shave off the kernels. Add to the chicken bowl and repeat with the other cob.

2 Stir the grated cheese, peppers, beans, onion, lettuce and some seasoning into the chicken bowl, adding as much lettuce as you like.

3 Put the soured cream and lime juice into a small bowl and stir together to make a dressing. Toss this through the salad and check the seasoning. Crunch the tortillas into the bowl, mix through and serve.

Serves 4

Beef Satay Salad

Hands-on time: 20 minutes
Cooking time: about 15 minutes

1 tbsp groundnut oil

500g (1lb 2oz) sirloin steaks, excess fat trimmed

2 shallots, thinly sliced

3 tbsp smooth peanut butter

150ml (¼ pint) coconut milk

finely grated zest and juice of 1 lime

2 × 70g packs of lamb's lettuce

200g (7oz) radishes, thinly sliced

a large handful of fresh coriander, roughly chopped

40g (1½oz) salted peanuts, chopped

½–1 red chilli, seeded and finely chopped, to taste (see Safety Tip, page 142)

salt and freshly ground black pepper

crusty bread to serve (optional)

1 Heat the oil in a large frying pan over medium-high heat. Season the steaks and add to the pan. Cook for 4 minutes, turning once, or until cooked to your liking. Transfer to a board, cover with foil and leave to rest.

2 Turn the heat under the pan down to low. Add the shallots to the pan and cook gently for 5 minutes or until softened. Stir in the peanut butter, coconut milk and lime zest and juice. Heat through and check the seasoning, adding a little water to thin it, if you like.

3 Empty the lamb's lettuce on to a large serving dish, add the radishes and coriander and toss through. Slice the beef and add it to the salad together with most of the peanuts and chilli. Toss together.

4 To serve, scatter the remaining peanuts and chilli over the salad and serve with the dressing on the side. Great with crusty bread to mop up the dressing.

Serves 4

Perfect Chillies and Garlic

Most of a chilli's heat resides in the seeds and white pith, so it is usually best to remove these, then finely chop or slice the flesh with care. Garlic has a pungent flavour and aroma and can be used raw to flavour dressings and butters, or fried at the beginning of savoury recipes.

Perfect chillies

1 Cut off the cap and slit open lengthways. Using a spoon, scrape out the seeds and the pith (the hottest parts of the chilli).
2 For diced chilli, cut into thin shreds lengthways, then cut crossways.

1

SAFETY TIP

Chillies vary enormously in strength, from quite mild to blisteringly hot, depending on the type of chilli and its ripeness. Taste a small piece first to check it's not too hot for you.
Be extremely careful when handling chillies not to touch or rub your eyes with your fingers, as they will sting. Always wash your hands thoroughly with soap and water immediately after handling chillies. Wash knives immediately after handling chillies for the same reason. As a precaution, use rubber gloves when preparing them, if you like.

Perfect garlic

1. Put the clove on the chopping board and put the flat side of a large knife on top of it. Press down firmly on the flat of the blade to crush the clove and break the papery skin.

2. Cut off the base of the clove and slip the garlic out of its skin. It should come away easily.

3. **Slicing** Using a rocking motion with the knife tip on the board, slice the garlic as thinly as you need.

4. **Shredding and chopping** Holding the slices together, shred them across the slices. Chop the shreds if you need chopped garlic.

5. **Crushing** After step 2, the whole clove can be put into a garlic press. To crush with a knife, roughly chop the peeled cloves and put them on the board with a pinch of salt.

6. **Puréeing** Press down hard with the edge of a large knife tip (with the blade facing away from you), then drag the blade along the garlic while still pressing hard. Continue to do this, dragging the knife tip over the garlic.

Chilli Beef Noodle Salad

🍴 **Hands-on time:** 15 minutes, plus soaking

150g (5oz) dried rice noodles
50g (2oz) rocket
125g (4oz) sliced cold roast beef
125g (4oz) sunblush tomatoes, chopped

For the Thai dressing

juice of 1 lime
1 lemongrass stalk, outside leaves discarded, trimmed and finely chopped
1 red chilli, seeded and chopped (see Safety Tip, page 142)
2 tsp finely chopped fresh root ginger
2 garlic cloves, crushed
1 tbsp Thai fish sauce
3 tbsp extra virgin olive oil
salt and freshly ground black pepper

1 Put the noodles into a large bowl and pour boiling water over them to cover. Put to one side for 15 minutes.
2 To make the dressing, whisk together the lime juice, lemongrass, chilli, ginger, garlic, fish sauce and oil in a small bowl and season with salt and ground black pepper.
3 While they are still warm, drain the noodles well, put into a large bowl and toss with the dressing. Leave to cool.
4 Just before serving, toss the rocket, sliced beef and tomatoes through the noodles.

SAVE EFFORT

An easy way to get a brand new dish is to use roast pork instead of beef.

Serves 4

The Ultimate Barbecue Sauce

To make 300ml (½ pint), you will need:

3 tbsp olive oil, 3 finely chopped garlic cloves, 3 tbsp balsamic vinegar, 4 tbsp dry sherry, 3 tbsp sun-dried tomato paste or tomato purée, 3 tbsp sweet chilli sauce, 300ml (½ pint) passata, 5 tbsp runny honey.

1 Put the oil, garlic, vinegar, sherry, tomato paste or purée and the chilli sauce into a bowl and mix well. Pour into a pan, then add the passata and honey.
2 Bring to the boil, then reduce the heat and simmer for 10–15 minutes until thick.

Avocado Salsa

To serve four to six, you will need:

3 large ripe tomatoes, 1 large red pepper, 2 small red chillies, 1 finely chopped red onion, 4 tbsp freshly chopped coriander, 2 tbsp freshly chopped parsley, 2 ripe avocados, salt and freshly ground black pepper.

1 Quarter, seed and dice the tomatoes. Core, seed and finely chop the pepper. Halve, seed and finely chop the chillies (see Safety Tip, page 142) and combine with the tomatoes, peppers, onion and herbs.
2 Halve, stone, peel and dice the avocados. Add to the salsa and season well with salt and ground black pepper. Toss well and serve within about 10 minutes. (Cut avocado flesh will discolour if left for longer than this.)

Mustard and Caper Sauce

Mash the yolks of 2 hard-boiled eggs with 2 tsp smooth Dijon mustard. Add 2 tbsp white wine vinegar and gradually whisk in 8 tbsp olive oil. Add 2 tbsp chopped capers, 1 tbsp chopped shallot and a pinch of sugar. Season with salt and freshly ground black pepper.

Almond and Herb Pesto

Put 50g (2oz) fresh flat-leafed parsley, 1 thick slice stale bread (crust removed), 2 tbsp lemon juice and 1–2 garlic cloves into a food processor and whiz to combine, then whiz in 50g (2oz) toasted almonds and 200ml (7fl oz) olive oil.

Flavoured butter

A pat of flavoured butter makes an instant sauce for simply grilled fish, chicken, meat or vegetables. You will need:
25g (1oz) soft unsalted butter per serving, plus flavouring (see below).

1 Beat the softened butter together with the flavouring. Turn out on to clingfilm, shape into a log and wrap tightly.
2 Chill in the fridge for at least 1 hour. Keep for up to one week (or freeze for up to one month).

Flavourings

For 125g (4oz) unsalted butter.
Anchovy butter: 6 mashed anchovy fillets.
Herb butter: 2 tbsp finely chopped herbs, a squeeze of lemon juice.
Garlic butter: 1 crushed garlic clove, 2 tsp finely chopped fresh parsley.

Hearty Salads

Make Your Own Mayo

The simplest of accompaniments, mayonnaise goes well with salads. Depending on your salad ingredients, you can flavour the basic mayonnaise with a variety of herbs, vegetables and fruit.

Mayonnaise

To make about 250ml (9fl oz), you will need:

2 large egg yolks, 1 tsp English mustard, 200ml (7fl oz) sunflower oil, 100ml (3½fl oz) extra virgin olive oil, 1 tsp white wine vinegar or lemon juice, salt and freshly ground black pepper.

1 Put the egg yolks into a 900ml (1½ pint) bowl. Stir in the mustard, 1 tsp salt and plenty of ground black pepper.

2 Combine the oils and add 1 tsp to the egg yolks. Whisk thoroughly, then add another 1 tsp and whisk until thickened. Continue adding about half the oil, 1 tbsp at a time. Whisk in the vinegar or lemon juice, then add the oil in a thin, steady stream until the mayonnaise is thick.

3 Check the seasoning, adding more vinegar or lemon juice if necessary. If not using immediately, cover and chill for up to four days.

Lemon and Garlic

To make about 150ml (¼ pint), you will need:
175ml (6fl oz) mayonnaise, 1 tbsp grated lemon zest plus 1 tbsp lemon juice, 2 finely chopped spring onions, 1 crushed garlic clove, salt and freshly ground black pepper.

1 Put all the ingredients into a medium bowl and beat well to combine. Check the seasoning.
2 If not using immediately, cover and chill for up to two days.

Smoky Pepper

To make about 175ml (6fl oz), you will need:
1 peeled and chopped grilled red pepper, 1 garlic clove, 250ml (9fl oz) mayonnaise, 2 tsp chilli oil, 2 tbsp lemon juice.

1 Put the red pepper, garlic and mayonnaise into a food processor and whiz to combine.
2 Stir in the chilli oil and lemon juice.
3 If not using immediately, cover and chill for up to two days.

Mango

To make about 175ml (6fl oz), you will need:
1 large peeled and stoned mango, 2 tsp freshly chopped coriander, 1 tsp peeled and grated fresh root ginger, juice of 1 lime, 200ml (7fl oz) sunflower oil, salt and freshly ground black pepper.

1 Mash the flesh of the mango in a bowl and add the coriander, ginger and lime juice. Season well with salt and ground black pepper.
2 Slowly whisk in the oil until the mayonnaise is thick.
3 If not using immediately, cover and chill for up to two days.

Warm Mussel, Leek and Herb Salad

Hands-on time: 10 minutes, plus chilling
Cooking time: about 10 minutes

700g (1½lb) trimmed baby leeks
juice of 1 lemon
½ tsp Dijon mustard
6 tbsp olive oil
4 tbsp roughly chopped fresh chervil
  or parsley
2 tbsp freshly chopped chives
900g (2lb) cooked mussels in the shell
  (see Save Effort)
salt and freshly ground black pepper
orange wedges to garnish

1 Cook the leeks in salted boiling water until just tender. Drain and refresh in ice-cold water. Drain and dry well on kitchen paper.

2 Put 2 tbsp lemon juice into a bowl, season with salt and ground black pepper and add the mustard. Whisk to combine, then whisk in the oil. Toss the leeks in a little of the dressing, then cover and chill.

3 Just before serving, mix the herbs into the reserved dressing. Reheat the mussels and pour the dressing over. Spoon the hot mussels over the leeks and serve garnished with orange wedges.

SAVE EFFORT

Ready-cooked, vacuum-packed mussels are available from most supermarkets.

Serves 4

Tarragon Turkey and Bean Salad

Hands-on time: about 20 minutes

2 tbsp roughly chopped fresh tarragon

2 tbsp roughly chopped fresh flat-leafed parsley

1 tbsp olive oil

2 tbsp crème fraîche

200ml (7fl oz) mayonnaise

juice of ½ lemon

450g (1lb) cooked turkey, cut into bite-size pieces

400g can cannellini beans, drained and rinsed

50g (2oz) sunblush or sun-dried tomatoes, roughly chopped

salt and freshly ground black pepper

finely sliced spring onion to garnish

For the shallot dressing

2 tbsp sunflower oil

1 tsp walnut oil

2 tsp red wine vinegar

1 small shallot, very finely chopped

a pinch of caster sugar

1 Put the herbs into a food processor and add the olive oil. Whiz until the herbs are chopped. Add the crème fraîche, mayonnaise and lemon juice to the processor and season with salt and ground black pepper, then whiz until well combined. Alternatively, chop the herbs by hand, mix with the oil, then beat in the crème fraîche, mayonnaise, lemon juice and seasoning. Toss the turkey with the herb dressing in a large bowl and put to one side.

2 To make the shallot dressing, whisk the ingredients together in a small bowl and season.

3 Tip the cannellini beans into a bowl, toss with the shallot dressing and season well. Arrange the cannellini beans in a serving dish. Top the beans with the dressed turkey and the tomatoes and garnish with spring onion.

Quick Caribbean Chicken Salad

Hands-on time: 10 minutes
Cooking time: about 20 minutes

4 chicken breast fillets, skin on
4 tsp jerk seasoning
450g (1lb) Jersey royal potatoes
100ml (3½fl oz) mayonnaise
2 tbsp wholegrain mustard
2 tbsp vegetable oil
1 red onion, cut into thin wedges
125g (4oz) brown cap mushrooms, halved
225g (8oz) young spinach leaves
3 tbsp freshly chopped chives
lemon juice to taste
salt and freshly ground black pepper

1 Heat the grill to maximum. Season the chicken breasts with salt and ground black pepper and rub with jerk seasoning. Grill the chicken for 5 minutes on each side or until cooked through. Put to one side.

2 Meanwhile, cook the potatoes in salted boiling water for 10 minutes or until tender. Drain, cool a little, then cut into chunks. Mix the mayonnaise and mustard together, then add to the potatoes, stir and put to one side.

3 Heat the oil in a large frying pan, add the onion and fry for 5 minutes. Add the mushrooms and cook for a further 2 minutes, then season with salt and ground black pepper.

4 Combine the potato and mushroom mixtures in a bowl and add the spinach and chives. Toss to combine, then add the lemon juice and season with salt and pepper. Cut the chicken into thick slices on the diagonal and serve with the salad.

SAVE EFFORT

An easy way to get a brand new dish is to replace the seasoned chicken with slices of smoked ham.

Serves 4

Crispy Duck Salad

Hands-on time: 30 minutes, plus overnight chilling
Cooking time: about 1½ hours, plus cooling

6 duck legs (each about 200g/7oz)
1 tsp peppercorns
2 fresh thyme sprigs
2 bay leaves
125g (4oz) pecan nuts
finely grated zest and juice of 2
   oranges
225g (8oz) cranberries
125g (4oz) caster sugar
4 tbsp white wine vinegar
9 tbsp sunflower oil
3 tbsp walnut oil
125g (4oz) kumquats, quartered
salt and freshly ground black pepper
salad leaves, such as frisée, to serve

1 Preheat the oven to 180°C (160°C fan oven) mark 4. Put the duck legs in a large flameproof casserole, cover with cold water and bring to the boil. Reduce the heat and simmer for 10 minutes, skim the surface of the liquid and add the peppercorns, thyme, bay leaves and 2 tsp salt. Transfer to the oven and cook for 45 minutes–1 hour until tender. Cool quickly in the liquid and chill in the fridge overnight.

2 Heat the grill. Put the pecan nuts on a baking sheet and grill lightly.

3 Put the orange zest in a frying pan with 200ml (7fl oz) of the orange juice, together with the cranberries and sugar. Bring to the boil, then reduce the heat and simmer gently for 5 minutes or until the cranberries are tender. Drain the cranberries, reserving the juice, and put to one side. Bring the juice to the boil, then reduce the heat and bubble until syrupy, then add the reserved cranberries. Put to one side.

4 Put a good pinch of salt and ground black pepper in a small bowl, then whisk in the vinegar, followed by the oils. Add the kumquats to the cranberry mixture with the dressing and pecans. Put to one side.

5 Skim the fat from the surface of the jellied duck liquid and put to one

side. Cut the duck into thick shreds, leaving the skin on.

6 Just before serving, heat 1 tbsp reserved duck fat in a large non-stick frying pan and fry half the duck for 5 minutes until very crisp and brown; leave in a warm place. Repeat with the remaining duck.

7 To serve, carefully toss the duck with the cranberry mixture and serve with salad leaves.

Spring Lamb and Flageolet Bean Salad

Hands-on time: 10 minutes
Cooking time: about 20 minutes, plus resting

2–3 lamb fillets (total weight about 700g/1½lb)

1 tbsp Dijon mustard

5 tbsp olive oil

1 tsp freshly chopped parsley

2 garlic cloves

juice of 1 lemon

400g can flageolet or cannellini beans, drained and rinsed

125g (4oz) frisée lettuce or curly endive

250g (9oz) baby plum or cherry tomatoes, halved

salt and freshly ground black pepper

1 Rub the lamb fillets with the mustard and season with ground black pepper. Put 1 tbsp of the oil into a non-stick frying pan and fry the lamb over a medium heat for 5–7 minutes on each side for medium-rare, 8–10 minutes for well done. Transfer the lamb to a warmed plate, cover and put to one side for 5 minutes. This allows the meat to relax, which makes slicing easier.

2 To make the dressing, put the parsley, garlic, lemon juice and remaining oil into a food processor and whiz for 10 seconds. Alternatively, put the ingredients into a screw-topped jar, screw on the lid and shake to combine.

3 Put the beans, frisée or curly endive and the tomatoes into a bowl, combine with the dressing and season to taste with salt and pepper.

4 Slice the lamb into 1cm (½in) pieces and place on top of the flageolet salad. Serve immediately.

Serves 4

Warm Chorizo and Chickpea Salad

Hands-on time: 15 minutes
Cooking time: about 20 minutes

5 tbsp olive oil

200g (7oz) chorizo or spicy sausage, thinly sliced

225g (8oz) red onion, chopped

1 large red pepper, seeded and roughly chopped

3 garlic cloves, finely chopped

1 tsp cumin seeds

2 × 400g cans chickpeas, drained and rinsed

2 tbsp freshly chopped coriander

juice of 1 lemon

salt and freshly ground black pepper

chilli oil to serve (optional, see Save Money)

SAVE MONEY

For an extra kick, drizzle 2 tbsp chilli oil over the salad. To make your own chilli oil, put 8 fresh or dried chillies and 600ml (1 pint) sunflower oil into a clean bottle, seal and leave for about two weeks. Strain into another clean bottle and use within six months.

1 Heat 1 tbsp of the olive oil in a non-stick frying pan and cook the chorizo or spicy sausage over a medium heat for 1–2 minutes or until lightly browned. Remove the chorizo with a slotted spoon and set aside. Fry the onion in the chorizo oil for 10 minutes or until browned.

2 Add the red pepper, garlic, cumin

162

and chickpeas to the onion and cook for a further 5 minutes, stirring frequently to prevent sticking. Take off the heat and add the chorizo.

3 Add the chopped coriander, lemon juice and remaining olive oil and season well. Drizzle with the chilli oil, if you like, and serve immediately. This salad is also delicious served cold.

Seared Beef Salad

Hands-on time: 10 minutes
Cooking time: about 4 minutes, plus resting

4 rump steaks
1 tbsp sunflower oil
125g (4oz) crème fraîche
3 tbsp horseradish
a squeeze of lemon juice
100g (3½oz) baby leaf spinach
150g (5oz) radishes, sliced
8 cherry tomatoes, halved
225g (8oz) cooked new potatoes, sliced
salt and freshly ground black pepper

1 Pat the steaks dry with kitchen paper, then season well on both sides. Heat a frying pan over a high heat until hot. Add the oil and turn the heat down to medium. Fry the steaks for 1½ minutes on each side for rare or 2 minutes on each side for medium, depending on the thickness of the slices. Cover loosely with foil and leave to rest for 5 minutes, then carve into thin slices.

2 Mix the crème fraîche with the horseradish, lemon juice and 1 tbsp warm water.

3 Arrange the beef slices in four bowls. Scatter with the spinach, radishes, tomatoes and sliced potatoes. Drizzle with the horseradish sauce and serve.

Serves 4

Italian-style Steak Salad

🍴 **Hands-on time:** 10 minutes
Cooking time: 10 minutes, plus resting

2 × 250g (9oz) rump steaks, fat trimmed

1 tbsp extra virgin olive oil, plus extra to drizzle (optional)

2–3 tbsp fresh pesto, to taste

110g bag salad leaves

250g (9oz) cherry tomatoes

100g (3½oz) marinated artichoke pieces from a jar, drained

50g (2oz) toasted pinenuts

25g (1oz) Parmesan, pared into shavings with a vegetable peeler

salt and freshly ground black pepper

crusty bread to serve

1 Pat the steaks dry with kitchen paper, then season well on both sides. Heat the oil in a large frying pan over a high heat and fry the steaks for 5 minutes, turning once, for medium rare (depending on the thickness of the slices, or as you prefer).

2 Meanwhile, put the pesto, some ground black pepper and enough water to make a loose dressing into a small bowl and stir together. Put the salad leaves, tomatoes and artichoke pieces into a large serving bowl, then pour most of the pesto dressing over and toss to combine.

3 When the steaks are cooked, transfer to a board and leave to rest for 5 minutes, then slice into strips. Add the steak strips to the salad, then drizzle the remaining pesto dressing over with some extra oil, if you like. Sprinkle the pinenuts and Parmesan shavings over the top and serve with crusty bread.

Serves 4

Deluxe Fig and Ham Salad

Hands-on time: 15 minutes
Cooking time: about 5 minutes

200g (7oz) trimmed fine green beans

3 tbsp extra virgin olive oil

4 slices white sourdough bread, cut
   into large cubes

4 Little Gem lettuces, quartered
   lengthways

85g pack of Parma ham

4 figs, quartered

1 tsp Dijon mustard

½ tbsp cider or white wine vinegar

salt and freshly ground black pepper

1 Bring a small pan of water to the boil
and cook the beans for 4 minutes
or until tender. Drain and leave in a
colander to steam-dry until needed.

2 Heat 1 tbsp of the oil in a large
frying pan and fry the bread cubes,
tossing frequently, until golden and
crisp. Season with salt and leave
to cool.

3 Arrange the lettuce quarters, cut
side up, on a large platter. Roughly
rip the Parma ham slices in half
lengthways and weave among the
lettuce quarters. Dot the figs, beans
and toasted bread cubes over the
ham and lettuce.

4 Put the Dijon mustard, vinegar,
remaining oil and some seasoning
into a small jug and whiz to
combine. Drizzle over the salad
and serve.

SAVE EFFORT

This decadent salad is perfect for a
dinner party. If you're not a fan of
figs, use peeled, stoned and sliced
fresh peaches.

168

364 cal ♥ 15g protein
9g fat (2g sat) ♥ 8g fibre
55g carb ♥ 2.1g salt

10

279 cal ♥ 10g protein;
6g fat (1g sat) ♥ 5g fibre
49g carb ♥ 0.2g salt

12

208 cal ♥ 7g protein
9g fat (trace sat) ♥ 3g fibre
28g carb ♥ 0g salt

14

193 cal ♥ 9g protein
8g fat (1g sat) ♥ 2g fibre
22g carb ♥ 0.3g salt

18

Calorie Gallery

192 cal ♥ 4g protein
1g fat (trace sat) ♥ 3g fibre
45g carb ♥ 0.1g salt

30

with 1 slice of cornbread
359 cal ♥ 25g protein
4g fat (1g sat) ♥ 6g fibre
64g carb ♥ 1.3g salt

32

137 cal ♥ 14g protein
9g fat (5g sat) ♥ 3g fibre
5g carb ♥ 0.4g salt

36

240 cal ♥ 16g protein
9g fat (2g sat) ♥ 3g fibre
25g carb ♥ 1.6g salt

48

205 cal ♥ 37g protein
4g fat (1g sat) ♥ 0.6g fibre
12g carb ♥ 0.4g salt

50

214 cal ♥ 12g protein
7g fat (1g sat) ♥ 10g fibre
29g carb ♥ 0.2g salt

56

132 cal ♥ 32g protein
2g fat (0g sat) ♥ 0.7g fibre
4g carb ♥ 1.4g salt

68

280 cal ♥ 22g protein
7g fat (2g sat) ♥ 3g fibre
34g carb ♥ 0.8g salt

70

298 cal ♥ 11g protein
4g fat (1g sat) ♥ 56g fibre
0.8g carb ♥ 8g salt

72

249 cal ♥ 10g protein
9g fat (4g sat) ♥ 1g fibre
31g carb ♥ 0.9g salt

78

145 cal ♥ 11g protein
1g fat (0g sat) ♥ 5g fibre
30g carb ♥ 0.4g salt

188 cal ♥ 4g protein
7g fat (1g sat) ♥ 3g fibre
29g carb ♥ 0g salt

156 cal ♥ 1g protein
0g fat ♥ 2g fibre
40g carb ♥ 0g salt

187 cal ♥ 3g protein
1g fat (0g sat) ♥ 6g fibre
47g carb ♥ 0.1g salt

without sour cream or
guacamole: 375 cal
36g protein ♥ 8g fat (2g sat) ♥
5g fibre ♥ 41g carb ♥ 2g salt

188 cal ♥ 28g protein
3g fat (0g sat) ♥ 4g fibre
13g carb ♥ 1.8g salt

334 cal ♥ 18g protein
8g fat (2g sat) ♥ 2g fibre
51g carb ♥ 3.5g salt

256 cal ♥ 29g protein
10g fat (5g sat) ♥ 6g fibre
14g carb ♥ 0.4g salt

280 cal ♥ 10g protein
10g fat (1g sat) ♥ 7g fibre
34g carb ♥ 1.3g salt

168 cal ♥ 20g protein
7g fat (1g sat) ♥ 1g fibre
8g carb ♥ 0.2g salt

142 cal ♥ 15g protein
3g fat (1g sat) ♥ 2g fibre
16g carb ♥ 0.2g salt

271 cal ♥ 40g protein
7g fat (2g sat) ♥ 2g fibre
12g carb ♥ 0.8g salt

164 cal ♥ 5g protein
8g fat (1g sat) ♥ 9g fibre
22g carb ♥ 2g salt

268 cal ♥ 35g protein
3g fat (trace sat) ♥ 2g fibre
37g carb ♥ 0.4g salt

223 cal ♥ 12g protein
10g fat (2g sat) ♥ 2g fibre
22g carb ♥ 1.4g salt

371 cal ♥ 25g protein
5g fat (1g sat) ♥ 5g fibre
43g carb ♥ 5g salt

20
22
26
28
38
40
42
46
58
62
64
66
82
86
88
90

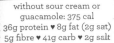

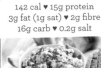

223 cal ♥ 17g protein
6g fat (2g sat) ♥ 1g fibre
30g carb ♥ 0.2g salt

92

331cal ♥ 28g protein
8g fat (2g sat) ♥ 1g fibre
37g carb ♥ 2g salt

96

393 cal ♥ 15g protein
9g fat (4g sat) ♥ 3g fibre
66g carb ♥ 0.3g salt

98

177 cal ♥ 13g protein
7g fat (3g sat) ♥ 1g fibre
16g carb ♥ 1.3g salt

100

207 cal ♥ 23g protein
10g fat (3g sat) ♥ 2g fibre
4g carb ♥ 2g salt

114

200 cal ♥ 6g protein
10g fat (2g sat) ♥ 5g fibre
19g carb ♥ 0.7g salt

116

103 cal ♥ 2g protein
4g fat (1g sat) ♥ 3g fibre
15g carb ♥ 0.1g salt

120

188 cal ♥ 15g protein
7g fat (2g sat) ♥ 2g fibre
15g carb ♥ 0.1g salt

132

193 cal ♥ 24g protein
5g fat (1g sat) ♥ 2g fibre
13g carb ♥ 1.2g salt

136

342 cal ♥ 9g protein
8g fat (4g sat) ♥ 1g fibre
61g carb ♥ 2g salt

138

392 cal ♥ 30g protein
5g fat (1g sat) ♥ 9g fibre
64g carb ♥ 4g salt

156

306 cal ♥ 13g protein
8g fat (2g sat) ♥ 10g fibre
44g carb ♥ 2.3g salt

158

130 cal ♥ 10g protein
2g fat (1g sat) ♥ 8g fibre
24g carb ♥ 0.3g salt

160

52 cal ♥ 0.9g protein
trace fat ♥ 1g fibre
13g carb ♥ 0g salt

162

Calorie Gallery

282 cal ♥ 29g protein
7g fat (1g sat) ♥ 4g fibre
29g carb ♥ 1.3g salt

102

3 skewers: 153 cal
14g protein ♥ 2g fat
(0.3g sat) ♥ 2g fibre
19g carb ♥ 0.8g salt

106

273 cal ♥ 42g protein
7g fat (2g sat) ♥ 3g fibre
9g carb ♥ 1g salt

108

201 cal ♥ 44g protein
2g fat (1g sat) ♥ 0.2g fibre
7g carb ♥ 0.5g salt

112

209 cal ♥ 30g protein
6g fat (1g sat) ♥ 4g fibre
6g carb ♥ 1.4g salt

122

171 cal ♥ 30g protein
1g fat (trace sat) ♥ 0.3g fibre
10g carb ♥ 0.8g salt

124

363 cal ♥ 25g protein
7g fat (2g sat) ♥ 6g fibre
54g carb ♥ 1g salt

126

203 cal ♥ 44g protein
4g fat (1g sat) ♥ 0.9g fibre
3g carb ♥ 1g salt

130

309 cal ♥ 14g protein
8g fat (3g sat) ♥ 11g fibre
51g carb ♥ 3g salt

140

281 cal ♥ 37g protein
10g fat (3g sat) ♥ 0.8g fibre
10g carb ♥ 1.3g salt

144

346 cal ♥ 44g protein
7g fat (3g sat) ♥ 0.4g fibre
28g carb ♥ 3g salt

152

264 cal ♥ 30g protein
8g fat (2g sat) ♥ 2g fibre
6g carb ♥ 0.2g salt

154

128 cal ♥ 3g protein
1g fat (trace sat) ♥ 3g fibre
30g carb ♥ 0.1g salt

164

147 cal ♥ 5g protein ♥ 1g fat
(trace sat) ♥ 8g fibre
33g carb ♥ 0g salt

166

205 cal ♥ 10g protein
3g fat (2g sat) ♥ 2g fibre
36g carb ♥ 0.3g salt

168

Index

PICTURE CREDITS
Photographers:
Steve Baxter (page 69); Nicki
Dowey (pages 11, 33, 37, 39, 41, 43,
47, 49, 51, 79, 93, 99, 101, 107, 113,
115, 117, 121, 123, 125, 129, 137, 145,
153, 155, 157, 159, 161, 163 and 165);
Gareth Morgans (pages 19, 23,
57, 65, 73, 91, 97, 103, 131 and 133);
Myles New (pages 13, 21 and 59);
Craig Robertson (pages 16, 17, 24,
25, 44, 80, 81, 84, 94, 95, 110, 111,
126, 127, 142, 143 and 150); Lucinda
Symons (pages 15, 27
and 29); Philip Webb (page 31);
Jon Whitaker (pages 63, 67, 71,
87, 109 and 167); Kate Whitaker
(pages 83, 78, 139, 141 and 169).

Home Economists:
Anna Burges-Lumsden, Joanna
Farrow, Emma Jane Frost, Teresa
Goldfinch, Alice Hart, Lucy
McKelvie, Kim Morphew, Aya
Nishimura, Bridget Sargeson,
Stella Sargeson, Sarah Tildesley,
Kate Trend, Jennifer White and
Mari Mererid Williams.

Stylists: Tamzin Ferdinando,
Wei Tang, Sarah Tildesley,
Helen Trent and Fanny Ward.

BAKE ME A CAKE
There's always time for cake

EASY PEASY MEALS
Easy meals for every day

LET'S DO BRUNCH
Mouth-watering meals to start your day

CHEAP EATS
Budget-busting ideas that won't break the bank

SALAD DAYS
Oh-so-fresh ideas for fabulous salads

Available online at store.anovabooks.com and from all good bookshops

POSH NOSH
Delicious recipes to impress your guests

PARTY FOOD
Delicious recipes to get the party started

SLOW STOPPERS
Slow-cooked meals packed with flavour

GREAT VEG
Inspired ideas for delicious veggie meals

AL FRESCO EATS
Easy grills, barbecues and picnics

ROAST IT
There's nothing better than a delicious roast

FLASH IN THE PAN
Spice up your noodles and stir-fries

GLUTEN-FREE AND EASY
Oh-so-good-for-you recipes that taste great

LOW FAT LOW CAL
Nice recipes don't need to be naughty